George Orwell Illustrated

George Orwell Illustrated

David Smith

Illustrated by
Mike Mosher

Haymarket Books
Chicago, Illinois

Text © 2018 and 1984 David Smith
Art © 2018 and 1984 Mike Mosher
Pages 12–198 originally appeared as Orwell for Beginners
(Writers and Readers Publishing Cooperative Ltd.)

Published in 2018 by
Haymarket Books
P.O. Box 180165
Chicago, IL 60618
773-583-7884
www.haymarketbooks.org
info@haymarketbooks.org

ISBN: 978-1-60846-783-9

Trade distribution:
In the US, Consortium Book Sales and Distribution, www.cbsd.com
In Canada, Publishers Group Canada, www.pgcbooks.ca
In the UK, Turnaround Publisher Services, www.turnaround-uk.com
All other countries, Ingram Publisher Services International, ips_intlsales@
ingramcontent.com

This book was published with the generous support of Lannan Foundation
and Wallace Action Fund.

Printed in Canada by union labor.

Library of Congress Cataloging-in-Publication data is available.

10 9 8 7 6 5 4 3 2 1

Love for Laura, and the whole clan:
Robin, Julia, Daniel, Paige, Laurie, Mike, Violet
. . . and the rest of my family and friends.
— DS

To Chrysanthe,
and Family
— MM

Contents

Preface

Orwell for Beginners

Planet Orwell

Acknowledgements

Thanks to Amy Reff, Daniel Smith, and Steve Stallone for design help, and thanks to Keith Rosenthal and Tony Feldmann for archival assistance at Harvard and the University of Chicago, respectively.

Readers will find a full bibliography, with credits for illustrations by artists besides Mike Mosher, posted at this online site: https://www.researchgate.net/profile/David_Smith366

Preface

Orwell in 2018

At the 1941 World Congress of PEN, Arthur Koestler surprised his friends by wagering five bottles of burgundy that George Orwell would be "the greatest best seller" within five years.

The setting for Koestler's prediction was apropos: PEN, founded 20 years earlier, was internationally active in defense of free speech, and Orwell, like Koestler, had begun to make a name for himself as an unyielding partisan of intellectual freedom.

But otherwise, Orwell was still little known.

Orwell's early novels and memoirs—including his autobiographical narrative of anti-fascist struggle during the Spanish Civil War, *Homage to Catalonia* (1938)—had won him only a modest readership.

His reputation as an incomparably lucid and truth-telling essayist was still in its infancy.

But Koestler, whose own most famous book, *Darkness at Noon*, had appeared just the year before, was soon proven right.

Animal Farm, Orwell's withering satire of the hollowing-out of the Russian revolution, won a global audience soon after it appeared in 1945. A year later—five years to the month after Koestler's wager—*Animal Farm* was named a Book-of-the-Month Club selection.

Although the Club's reviewer was less than eloquent—*Animal Farm*, he said, is a "semi-brilliant book on pig life and dictators"—his prediction that *Animal Farm* is an "English success [which would soon be] an American success" —was prescient.

Before long, the Book-of-the-Month Club edition of *Animal Farm* had sold nearly a half-million copies. Two other English editions flew off the shelves, and translations into many languages ensued.

And then came *Nineteen Eighty-Four*.

Novelist Robert Harris may have been guilty of exaggeration when he called Orwell's bleak dystopia "the most influential book ever written." But Orwell's influence has pulsed around the globe with increasing velocity ever since *Nineteen Eighty-Four* first appeared in 1949.

When whistleblower Edward Snowden revealed in 2013 that the National Security Agency was engaging in massive, illegal domestic surveillance, sales of *Nineteen Eighty-Four* rose 5,771%. And Snowden's ensuing exile dramatized the global reach of the security state.

In 2017, when one of the new president's top advisers endorsed "alternative facts," *Nineteen Eighty-Four* rose to the top of Amazon's bestseller list.

Koestler's prediction now seems almost understated. Orwell's searing warnings are as fresh as the headlines. Every day we see new evidence of the power of the "Orwellian vision— great powers with greater weapons and endless small wars; ruthless police states with disinformation as policy; soul-killing regimentation..."

The Path to Planet Orwell

Eric Blair did not live to see his pen name, "George Orwell," become a household name. Gravely ill when he finished *Nineteen Eighty-Four*, the 46-year-old Orwell died in January 1950, just months after his tale first appeared in print. His early death made the interpretation of the novel—which was controversial from the start—all the more difficult. Many critics saw the book as a merciless attack on socialism. Others said that Orwell's message applied to authoritarian regimes of every kind. Some readers heard a cry of despair; others heard a call to action, a call to abandon illusions, a roaring alarm.

Orwell himself, seeing the first green shoots of the debate sprout before his eyes, said that his intention with *Nineteen Eighty-Four* was neither to surrender to despair nor to repudiate the socialist ethic of freely shared wealth and power. That ethic had been at the center of all his writing, and it remained a source of living inspiration, even as he descended imaginatively into the hellscape of *Nineteen Eighty-Four*'s "Oceania" and "Airstrip One," where the power-mad O'Brien tormented the rebel everyman Winston Smith both physically and philosophically.

Orwell's early death stilled his prophetic voice just as *Nineteen Eighty-Four* was becoming the book that launched a thousand interpretations. That left the field of debate open—to everyone, that is, except Orwell himself. But Orwell had speculated aloud in a similar spirit, in 1945, about the prodigal writer and adventurer Jack London. Where would London have landed on the political map if he had not died young in 1916? If he had lived until 1945, he would then have been 69—and he would have witnessed the Russian revolution, the rise and fall of fascism and Nazism, the Great Depression, the New Deal, and the Labour Party's victory in Britain in 1945.

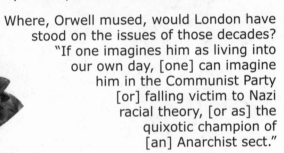

Where, Orwell mused, would London have stood on the issues of those decades? "If one imagines him as living into our own day, [one] can imagine him in the Communist Party [or] falling victim to Nazi racial theory, [or as] the quixotic champion of [an] Anarchist sect."

For many observers Orwell has been similarly Sphinx-like. He was less chameleon-like than London, so that, on the whole, speculation about his ultimate tendencies has been less extreme. But Wyndham Lewis did once casually surmise that the violently anti-totalitarian Orwell would have been a Nazi if he had been German —a guess at variance with everything we know about Orwell, who volunteered to fight fascism in the Spanish Civil War and afterwards fought authoritarianism in every form. And even Lewis, who wrote a pro-Hitler book before he wrote an anti-Hitler book, did not suggest that Orwell would have been a proponent of Nazi racial theory.

Nonetheless, tensions in Orwell's worldview have often raised questions. I discuss many of those tensions in in part 1 of this book, "Orwell for Beginners," which first appeared in 1984, and I report newer findings in part 2, "Planet Orwell."

Among those newer findings, the most notable is a never-before-published document, "Orwell's Manifesto," coauthored with Arthur Koestler and Bertrand Russell, which I found in an obscure archive in early 2017.

That manifesto sheds new light on his personality and politics—and suggests the question:

What if Orwell had lived to be 80?

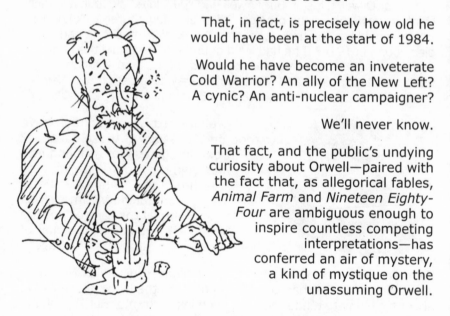

That, in fact, is precisely how old he would have been at the start of 1984.

Would he have become an inveterate Cold Warrior? An ally of the New Left? A cynic? An anti-nuclear campaigner?

We'll never know.

That fact, and the public's undying curiosity about Orwell—paired with the fact that, as allegorical fables, *Animal Farm* and *Nineteen Eighty-Four* are ambiguous enough to inspire countless competing interpretations—has conferred an air of mystery, a kind of mystique on the unassuming Orwell.

A paragon of plain speaking, Orwell has also become a riddle shrouded in mystery wrapped in an enigma.

His gaunt image has become a kind of political Rorschach test, tempting observers to see in him what they wish to see.

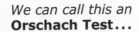

We can call this an
Orschach Test...

Upon reading *Animal Farm*,
the literary critic William Empson,
who had worked with Orwell at
the BBC during World War II,
told him:

"You must expect to be
'misunderstood' on a large scale."

Misunderstood he was.

When, in July 1949, *Life* magazine ran a feature story on
Nineteen Eighty-Four, which had appeared just the month
before—"The Strange World of 1984," lavishly illustrated by
Abner Dean—the accompanying editorial set the tone for many
future interpretations:

THIRTY-FIVE YEARS HENCE

Orwell predicts tyranny unlimited if we don't resist.

For *Life*, Orwell's parable was an invitation to celebrate
American success. "What American, reveling in a standard of
living that makes the old kings impoverished by comparison,
can fully conceive of a world so tawdry?"

Communism was also a predictable foil: "Behind the Iron Curtain, if
the book can ever be smuggled there, the completely regimented and
fear-ridden world of 1984 will not seem strange or imaginative at all."

Life's editors also sneered at "do-good psychology"—how this epithet could apply to the power-hungry sadists of Big Brother's Oceania is unclear—which, they said, is taking "queer and ominous forms."

Henry Luce's *Life* magazine, of course, was famously reactionary. So portraying *Nineteen Eighty-Four* as a sweeping indictment of even the mildest philanthropy was entirely in character. That Orwell was both a stern anti-totalitarian and a convinced socialist was evidently beyond *Life*'s ken. His deep conviction that socialism is the highest form of democracy was either too subtle, or too radical, for *Life*'s editors.

They simply defended the conventional wisdom and the status quo, on the grounds that we can hope for nothing better.

Orwell was less conventional, and more hopeful. He believed it was possible to navigate *between* the treacherous shoals of capitalism and communism—to achieve a truly democratic society, ruled neither by the profit motive nor by a dictatorial elite—and that was, in fact, precisely what he sought to achieve throughout his life.

Fast-Forward to the Present

In 1984, the conventional wisdom about Orwell was undisturbed. *Animal Farm* was widely read as a parable about the folly of utopian hope. Revolutions, it was said, lead only from one elite to another. And *Nineteen Eighty-Four* was seen as the ultimate Cold War novel, showing the bureaucratic rigor mortis of Communism with unmatched clarity. The nuclear arms race was still at fever pitch, and the danger of war between the US and the USSR remained very grave.

Now, however, Communism is a fading memory. Russia and China remain authoritarian, but they have also embraced the profit motive.

And yet, Orwell's disturbing vision remains as unforgettable as ever. As he had wished, *Nineteen Eighty-Four* now appears to be a critique not of stereotyped "Communism" but of all antidemocratic politics. And there is a special irony in the fact that the NSA, the CIA, and other security services now loom large in charges of "Orwellian" abuses of power. Just years after Orwell's death, the CIA financed a worldwide effort to make *Animal Farm* and *Nineteen Eighty-Four* into ideological weapons of the Cold War.

A seriocomic effort to capture *Animal Farm* for the anti-Communist crusade resulted, in 1954, in an animated film that CIA censors had painstakingly vetted, seeking to delete every hint—of which there were many—that Orwell saw the 1917 revolution as a revolution betrayed, not as proof that revolutions must and can only fail.

Even at that early stage, the powers-that-be took Orwell seriously; and since then, they have often tried to deflect or neutralize Orwell's challenges. But the imaginative power of Orwell's vision continues to ensnare them. His writings are too piercingly and comprehensively critical to be easily domesticated. It is perhaps telling that, in 2012, Joan Bakewell of the Labour Party reported that the BBC had turned down the gift of an Orwell statue by Martin Jennings, even though Orwell was, and remains, the BBC's most famous alumnus.

"Apparently," she reflected, "George Orwell would be perceived as too left-wing a figure for the BBC to honour."

But, as it happened, Orwell is also too popular to ignore—precisely because his razor-sharp vision continues to resonate. In August 2016, the BBC confirmed that a life-sized bronze sculpture of Orwell would, in fact, be placed at the entrance to the BBC's new Broadcasting House.

An apt quote accompanied
the preliminary model of
the sculpture:

*IF LIBERTY MEANS
ANYTHING AT ALL,
IT MEANS THE RIGHT
TO TELL PEOPLE
WHAT THEY DO NOT
WANT TO HEAR.*

Decades after 1984, Orwell is still making waves.

He makes overreaching officials
and prying security services nervous.

The goal of this book is to explain why.

Orwell for Beginners

Politics

Few writers have been as influential—or as inadequately under-stood—as George Orwell.

Orwell's influence is unmistakable. Several key terms from his works— *1984*, *doublethink*, *Big Brother*—belong to the public domain, and his very name is a journalistic commonplace. The phrase "Orwellian"—applied to an idea or a regime—has the same emotional impact for this generation that the term "Machiavellian" had for previous generations.

Picture a vast, icy, impersonal police-state with a hateful ideology: this is the so-called Orwellian vision—a vision, it now seems, of mythic dimensions and lasting currency.

Above all, George Orwell's influence is political. The two great novels upon which his reputation rests—*Animal Farm* and *1984*—are both entirely political.

Slender, deftly-etched *Animal Farm* is a barbed parable of the 1917 Russian Revolution and its aftermath, with a cautionary moral: that the new regime, Stalin's, is just as tyrannical as its Tsarist precursor; that the Bolshevik revolution, like the French revolution of 1789, fell victim to a Napoleonic dictator.

1984 is even more sweeping: a ferocious satire on all forms of "totalitarian" power and culture, with a clear reference, again, to the Stalinist oligarchy in the Soviet Union. But Stalinism is hardly the only target of Orwell's withering critique in *1984*. Fascism and capitalism are also indicted. This is a point on which Orwell is widely misunderstood.

The popular impression is that, more than anything else, George Orwell sounded a warning against Communism; that Soviet Russia is the unique object of Orwell's scorn for tyrants; in brief, that Orwell perfected an equation linking socialism and dictatorship.

The reality is quite different. George Orwell *did* unmask Soviet Russia—not as socialist, however, but as a dictatorial parody of socialism.

Personally, Orwell was passionately pro-socialist. In 1937 he fought in the Spanish civil war in a revolutionary contingent organized by the non-Stalinist POUM (the Workers' Party for Marxist Unification).

From January until June 1937—until shot in the throat— Orwell joined anarchist and socialist workers resisting Fascist armies sponsored by Hitler and Mussolini. Fascism did, ultimately, win, but the indelible impression Orwell received was not of defeat, but of future revolutionary possibilities . . .

George Orwell felt that he had seen the future—and that it worked. A panorama of worker creativity, solidarity, and decency had unfolded before Orwell's eyes, giving him hope, for the first time, that radically democratic socialism is possible.

The circumstances which had permitted Fascism to defeat the revolutionary Spanish syndicalists would not recur inevitably in the future. Next time, or the time after, the workers might win.

After recovering from his war injuries Orwell resumed the writing career he had started, in 1927, upon leaving the Imperial Police in Burma at the age of 24. His excellent early books—*Burmese Days*, *The Road to Wigan Pier*—revealed a definite sympathy for the oppressed, English coalminers as well as Burmese peasants. But not until returning from Spain did Orwell become a "political writer" in the full, self-conscious sense.

omage to Catalonia, Coming Up for Air, Animal Farm, and *1984* are the principal books written between 1937 and Orwell's early death in 1950. Together with a stream of wonderful essays, these books are Orwell's testament.

In a sense, though, Orwell's legacy is greater than the sum of his books and essays. What Orwell taught— and demonstrated—is a compelling moral approach to political writing.

What did Orwell teach? Above all, that liberty without exploitation will not be attained by deception; that freedom requires truthfulness. Either people are pushed around—at work or by politicians—or they rule themselves.

It serves no democratic purpose to pretend that "liberation" is anything less than self-rule. The glittering dialectic of so-called "orthodox Marxist" rhetoric is false, for example, when it is used to justify dictatorship "in the name of the workers." Also bankrupt is the "democratic" rhetoric which claims liberty for a capitalist society ruled, in reality, by big business and the profit-motive.

If people are to be free, they must face facts and decide for themselves what must be done. Inquisitors *never* promote freedom. "Benevolent dictators" . . . are dictators.

Minute by minute, day by day, the public must know its chances and choices. No one can "help" the public by editing, cutting, and censoring the facts. If unpalatable truths and uncomfortable views are not *faced*, the public is disarmed before its enemies.

Is it helpful to underestimate an opponent?
To mistake a foe for a friend?
To call war peace?
To call slavery freedom?

Above all, *hard* truths must be faced. The only alternative is a public so ill-informed and misguided that rule by "experts" is inevitable.

NATIONAL "EVERYTHING IS OK" WEEK...

RELEASE
SECRET
TOP SECRET
CLASSIFY

WAR DEAD
LATEST FIGURES

DEPARTMENT OF PUBLIC
VERITAS

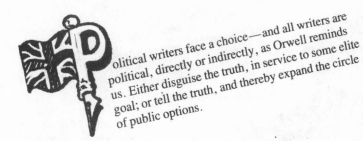

olitical writers face a choice—and all writers are political, directly or indirectly, as Orwell reminds us. Either disguise the truth, in service to some elite goal; or tell the truth, and thereby expand the circle of public options.

If Big Brother's new clothes are less resplendent than they are said to be, what should we say? Should we admire the imaginary velvet glove, and disregard the iron fist? Or should we point out the link between imaginary democratic raiment and police-state realities?

MAGNIFIQUE!

THIS YEAR'S SENSATION!

BUT HE'S BARENAKED!

When propaganda and the facts are discordant, Orwell counsels *saying so*.

Though personally he would have preferred to live "under the spreading chestnut tree" in a quieter era without Big Brothers and thought-police—as an Anglican poet, he said—Orwell felt that given world conflict and the danger of total war, political truth must ring out in clear, graceful, unpretentious language. This was his goal.

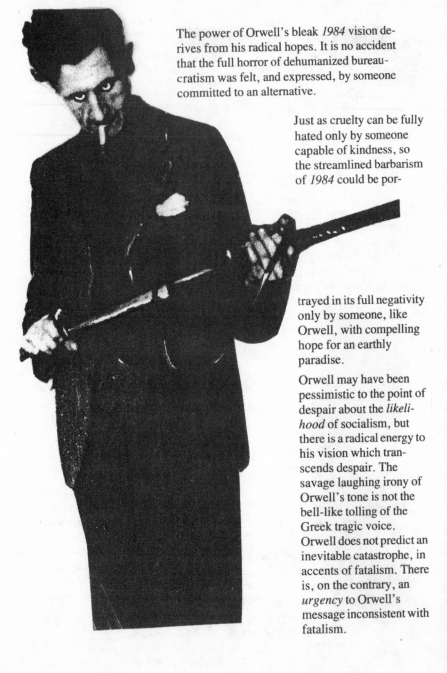

The power of Orwell's bleak *1984* vision derives from his radical hopes. It is no accident that the full horror of dehumanized bureaucratism was felt, and expressed, by someone committed to an alternative.

Just as cruelty can be fully hated only by someone capable of kindness, so the streamlined barbarism of *1984* could be por-

trayed in its full negativity only by someone, like Orwell, with compelling hope for an earthly paradise.

Orwell may have been pessimistic to the point of despair about the *likelihood* of socialism, but there is a radical energy to his vision which transcends despair. The savage laughing irony of Orwell's tone is not the bell-like tolling of the Greek tragic voice. Orwell does not predict an inevitable catastrophe, in accents of fatalism. There is, on the contrary, an *urgency* to Orwell's message inconsistent with fatalism.

The dark future which Orwell projects is not so much a prediction as a warning. Big Brother will not *inevitably* rule, but he *may*. *Newspeak* will not inevitably oust free thinking—but it might. Workers *might* be reduced to "proles," dissidents to "unpersons."

This dire fate can be averted. Weak reeds like Winston Smith in *1984* may be broken, but others—workers, dissidents—have the power to resist and win. *1984* was written not as an act of quietism and hopelessness, but as a stimulus to preventive action.

Orwell *cares* about "1984" while writing in 1948 because he believes that superpower wars, total police-states, and global misery *can be averted*. The hope may be slender—but what else merits attention? For Orwell, the alternative to the dementia of *1984* is not more of the desperately ill present—the very present which leads to 1984— but *socialism*, free cooperation between equals.

WE ALL KNOW WHAT ORWELL FEARED.
LET'S TURN, FOR A MOMENT, TO THE
SOCIALIST HOPES WHICH MADE THESE
FEARS SEEM SO MONSTROUS.

According to H.G. Wells, George Orwell was "a Trotskyite with big feet." Is this accurate?

Yes and no. Yes—Orwell had monumental feet. But no—Orwell was not, strictly speaking, a "Trotskyite."

Trotsky definitely did play a big role in Orwell's political thinking. Little disguised, Trotsky is a major figure in both *Animal Farm* and *1984*—as Snowball, the revolutionary pig vanquished by his former comrade, Napoleon, in *Animal Farm;* and as Immanuel Goldstein, Big Brother's only rival, in *1984*. In each case, Trotsky is portrayed as a basically sympathetic character, while Napoleon/Big Brother is depicted as certifiably evil.

This is reasonable, since Trotsky was a figure of heroic proportions—the leading public figure of the Bolshevik revolution, organizer of the Red Army, later (exiled by Stalin for urging a more revolutionary, democratic policy) the founder of an international opposition to Stalinism. Stalin, by contrast, was little more than a small-minded party functionary magnified on the world stage by his success in appropriating dictatorial power.

George Orwell turned to politics in 1935–36, just as Stalin moved to consolidate power in Russia and in the world Communist movement. Lenin had died in 1924. Trotsky had been exiled in 1928. Since then, Stalin had presided over a forced industrial revolution.

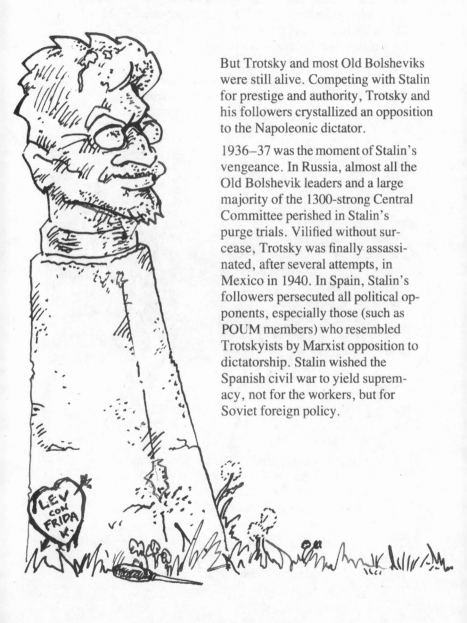

But Trotsky and most Old Bolsheviks were still alive. Competing with Stalin for prestige and authority, Trotsky and his followers crystallized an opposition to the Napoleonic dictator.

1936–37 was the moment of Stalin's vengeance. In Russia, almost all the Old Bolshevik leaders and a large majority of the 1300-strong Central Committee perished in Stalin's purge trials. Vilified without sur-cease, Trotsky was finally assassinated, after several attempts, in Mexico in 1940. In Spain, Stalin's followers persecuted all political opponents, especially those (such as POUM members) who resembled Trotskyists by Marxist opposition to dictatorship. Stalin wished the Spanish civil war to yield supremacy, not for the workers, but for Soviet foreign policy.

In the midst of war, the Spanish Republic accepted Soviet guidance as the price of arms. POUM members and Anarchists were ruthlessly persecuted. George Orwell evaded the dragnet, leaving Spain in June 1937. At roughly the same moment the grotesque Russian purge trials reached their zenith. Trotsky survived a few years longer, far and away the outstanding old Bolshevik opponent of the new Stalinist regime. His followers were active in many countries . . .

Orwell was never a Trotskyist, because he did not accept Trotsky's view that Stalinism was the result of Iosif Djugashvili's personal perfidy. ("Stalin,"

Orwell—
one of the
survivors

man of steel, was Djugashvili's *nom de guerre.*) Orwell felt that the same tendency to authoritarianism—the same softness towards dictatorial hardness—was evident in early Bolshevism, too.

Trotsky was unmistakably the mortal enemy of the Napoleonic *dictator,* but Trotsky never relinquished the idea of the disciplined, centralized party which would lead the workers.

Orwell mistrusted this idea greatly. Hence, "Goldstein" in *1984*—Trotsky's real name was Lev Davidovich Bronstein—is portrayed as a valiant opponent of Big Brother's, but from *within* the *Newspeak* traditions of the party. The implication is that Trotsky and Stalin were brothers under the skin . . . indeed, *"big brothers"* under the skin.

This view—to be discussed later—led Orwell to take a very critical stance towards Trotsky and Trotskyism. Still, Orwell was very much influenced by Trotsky, too.

This is not surprising at all, since Trotsky and his followers *did* oppose Stalin in the name of workers' democracy. Probably the most effective contemporary critique of the Napoleonic party dictatorship was Trotsky's *The Revolution Betrayed*, published in 1935 at the juncture of Orwell's swing to socialism—the model, evidently, for Emmanuel Goldstein's *Theory of Oligarchical Collectivism* in *1984*. And several of Trotsky's followers evolved even more challenging critiques of Bolshevism and its results.

Several vital if underpublicized currents of anarchism and libertarian Marxism developed in tandem with Orwell in the 1940s. This is highly relevant for our understanding of Orwell—since Orwell formed his ideas *in communication* and *in solidarity* with his fellow revolutionary democrats.

The key question under discussion at this time was the character of Soviet Russian society. Trotsky insisted that, though "deformed" by bureaucratic rule, Russia remained a workers' state. Orwell and others insisted, on the contrary, that no "workers' state" exists without power in the hands of the workers.

Whatever Soviet Russia may be— Orwell favored the term "oligarchical collectivism"—it will not be socialist (*i.e., democratic* collectivist) until workers rule directly and democratically. This will very likely require a second revolution . . .

The early protagonists in these still-relevant debates are now virtually unknown. Schools of thought which influenced Orwell—to which he belonged, in many ways—were several in number:

Free-thinking socialists of the POUM and Independent Labour Party tradition (*e.g.*, Andrés Nin, James Maxton); such creative ex-Trotskyists as C.L.R. James, Dwight McDonald, Max Schachtman, and James Burnham; anarchists like Herbert Read and Vernon Richards; radical writers like Victor Serge, Arthur Koestler, and Ignazio Silone; and scintillating left critics of "authoritarianism," including Wilhelm Reich, Erich Fromm, and Theodor Adorno.

Several of these writers are still well-known, but most are utterly neglected—and the libertarian socialist thinking to which they contributed is forgotten. Orwell, as a result, seems eccentric and isolated. Ill-informed critics, assuming that "all real socialists" endorse Stalinism, say that Orwell "spent more time criticizing socialism than defending it." Not so! The truth is that Orwell opposed *class rule*—tyranny—*in every form*. The only way to defend socialism with real integrity, he felt, is to oppose pseudo-socialism *as well* as capitalism.

Critics thus do Orwell a major injustice when they portray him as a wavering and uncertain idealist of doubtful socialist authenticity. What one biographer calls the *"Time-Life* and *Encounter"* version of Orwell's politics is the claim that Orwell was a quirky, light-minded utopian— a visionary Don Quixote, to be pitied for his radical diatribes while meriting applause for his anti-Communism.

TYPICALLY, ORWELL IS POR-TRAYED AS AN IDIOSYNCRATIC MAN OF SPECIAL "INCONSISTENCIES" WHO COULD NEVER FULLY BRING HIMSELF TO ACCEPT THE PECULIAR NON-STALINIST "SOCIALISM" HE AVOWED...

Yes, Orwell was a man of serious inconsistencies. But these inconsistencies were typical not just of Orwell, as an eccentric to be psychoanalyzed . . .

Ah yes, the Don Quixote complex, doubtless due to his big feet which give him cause to rage against the world . . .!

. . . but of the larger socialist current to which Orwell belonged.

In his basic values, in his wish for a free socialism based on friendship and decency, Orwell never wavered. But like many others—Koestler, Schachtman, Reich, *et al.*—Orwell grew progressively more pessimistic about the *capacity* of the working class to "emancipate itself" (in Marx's phrase). This led him to wonder whether international socialism is really possible—whether it is possible to stay free of the claims of Moscow, Washington, etc. If no *real* emancipation is possible, perhaps "lesser evils" are desirable? This is where Orwell wavered—on the *hope* for freedom . . .

With greater evils on the horizon—totalitarian police-states, nuclear war—Orwell and his peers debated several lesser evils:

> Is a weak, reformist labor party preferable to a potentially dictatorial revolutionary party?
>
> If socialism is not possible, is Stalinism better or worse than capitalism? Is either preferable?

On these questions Orwell vacillated. Sometimes he took positions he later repudiated, or which now seem strange. But even in error, Orwell represented the best and most sophisticated free socialism of his time. And Orwell's views are *still germane,* whether accurate or flawed. Anyone who aspires to freedom without private property faces the same issues. They remain unresolved. George Orwell is still vital because he addresses these questions with intelligence, courage, and integrity.

21

"George Orwell"—radical iconoclast—was originally Eric Blair, Eton-educated scion of the imperial English ruling class.

At one point an imperial policeman in Burma, Eric Blair later became a world-renowned enemy of police-state rule. How? Orwell's biographers and critics give conflicting testimony. Several key questions are debated:

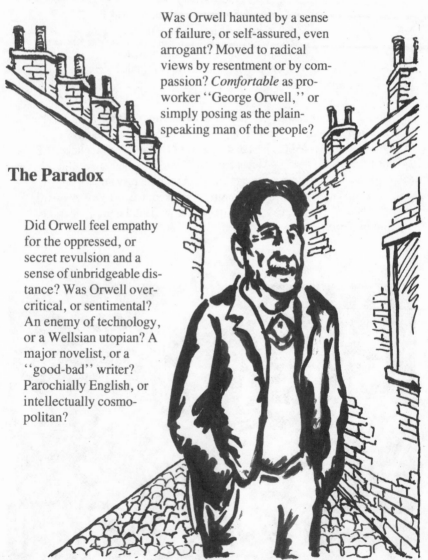

Was Orwell haunted by a sense of failure, or self-assured, even arrogant? Moved to radical views by resentment or by compassion? *Comfortable* as pro-worker "George Orwell," or simply posing as the plain-speaking man of the people?

The Paradox

Did Orwell feel empathy for the oppressed, or secret revulsion and a sense of unbridgeable distance? Was Orwell over-critical, or sentimental? An enemy of technology, or a Wellsian utopian? A major novelist, or a "good-bad" writer? Parochially English, or intellectually cosmopolitan?

Often, the paradoxes and uncertainties of Orwell's life are used against him. When Orwell is accused of bitterness, self-doubt, etc., his ideas are trivialized.

Even Orwell's greatest strengths are turned against him. Not an abstruse writer, Orwell was not, "therefore," a complex thinker. Not doctrinaire, Orwell was "eccentric." Not disposed to hide his biases, Orwell was actuated *only* by prejudice.

Why is Orwell so often caricatured? Principally, because he held exceptionally unorthodox views —views unpalatable to almost all critics. Orwell is not simply *ignored* thanks to his immense popularity as a prophetic novelist. But very few critics take Orwell's ideas seriously on their own terms. Few *confront* Orwell. The preferred strategy is *ad hominem*—innuendo instead of debate. For this purpose, Orwell's life appears as a field of ammunition to be used against him.

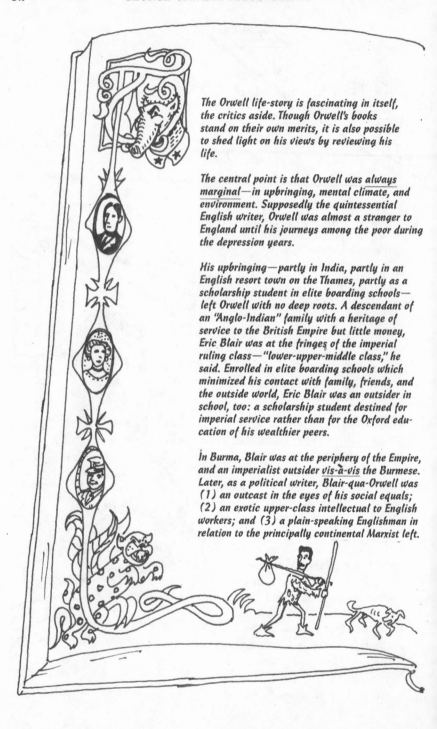

The Orwell life-story is fascinating in itself, the critics aside. Though Orwell's books stand on their own merits, it is also possible to shed light on his views by reviewing his life.

The central point is that Orwell was always marginal—in upbringing, mental climate, and environment. Supposedly the quintessential English writer, Orwell was almost a stranger to England until his journeys among the poor during the depression years.

His upbringing—partly in India, partly in an English resort town on the Thames, partly as a scholarship student in elite boarding schools— left Orwell with no deep roots. A descendant of an "Anglo-Indian" family with a heritage of service to the British Empire but little money, Eric Blair was at the fringes of the imperial ruling class—"lower-upper-middle class," he said. Enrolled in elite boarding schools which minimized his contact with family, friends, and the outside world, Eric Blair was an outsider in school, too: a scholarship student destined for imperial service rather than for the Oxford education of his wealthier peers.

In Burma, Blair was at the periphery of the Empire, and an imperialist outsider vis-à-vis the Burmese. Later, as a political writer, Blair-qua-Orwell was (1) an outcast in the eyes of his social equals; (2) an exotic upper-class intellectual to English workers; and (3) a plain-speaking Englishman in relation to the principally continental Marxist left.

All this, combined, gave Orwell his irony, his independence, and his critical distance from established shibboleths—his unique voice. In more ways than one, "George Orwell" was heir to no fixed traditions. He was self-made.

The contours of Orwell's life are simple: Born in India in 1903, Orwell entered boarding school in 1911. After completing his education in 1921, he entered the Imperial Police in Burma, serving until 1927. After leaving Burma, Orwell started to write, working odd jobs in France and England. By 1935, Orwell had completed three novels and had adopted his pen name. In 1936, he wrote his first political "documentary" (on English coalminers and socialism) and married Eileen O'Shaughnessy. In 1937, the Orwells fought with the POUM in Spain. Thereafter, with the exception of brief visits to Morocco and Germany, Orwell lived permanently in England. His literary output between 1937 and his early death in 1950 was extensive: 3000 pages of essays and journalism, several documentary books, BBC broadcasts during the Second World War, and three political novels.

A respiratory ailment dating back to his childhood (and aggravated by problems in Burma and elsewhere) led to Orwell's 1950 death by tuberculosis. Eileen O'Shaughnessy had died in 1945 and Orwell had married a second time in 1949, to Sonia Brownell. An adopted son from Orwell's first marriage—Richard—grew up to be a farmer.

To get the full flavor of Eric Blair's early
life, attention to his colonial background is
crucial. Allegiance to that background—
until it "outraged his nature" beyond the
breaking point—is the central theme of the
first half of Orwell's life.

Eric's father, Richard Walmsley Blair,
was the epitome of the petty imperial
bureaucrat. In 1875, 15 years after the
start of the opium trade with China,
Richard Blair entered imperial service
as an 18-year-old Assistant Sub-
Deputy Opium Agent—not *exactly* the
highest position available, but a start.

Richard Blair was nearly 40 when he
married Ida Limouzin in 1896. A
daughter, Marjorie, was born in 1898.
When Eric was born in June, 1903, in
the city of Motihari, Bengal, Richard
Blair was 46 and a Sub-Deputy Opium
Agent, Fourth Grade. By the date of
his retirement in 1912, Blair had risen
to the stellar level of a Sub-Deputy
Opium Agent, first grade. He had spent
37 years in the Indian Civil Service,
active in thirteen Indian communities.

Richard Blair's record in the Indian Civil Service was respectable, but a definite step down from his family's tradition. His great-grandfather, Charles, 1743–1802, had owned substantial property in Jamaica—"Estates, Plantations, Messuages, Tenements, and Heriditaments," according to his will.

Richard's father, Thomas, was less wealthy, but nevertheless served as an Anglican Vicar in Dorset. (He had been ordained by the Bishop of Calcutta, thus setting a family precedent of Indian service.)

Eric's mother, Ida Limouzin, belonged to a family substantially wealthier than the Blairs, and with more extensive Far East connections.

G. E. Limouzin, a French shipbuilder and teak merchant who died in 1863, had been a leading businessman in Moulmein, Burma, which named a street after him. His daughter-in-law, Ida's mother, was still living in Burma when Eric Blair served there as a policeman.

IDA LIMOUZIN BLAIR LIVED IN BURMA UNTIL HER MARRIAGE AT 21, THEN LIVED WITH RICHARD BLAIR IN INDIA UNTIL, IN 1904, SHE BROUGHT HER TWO CHILDREN TO ENGLAND.

A THIRD CHILD, AVRIL, WAS BORN IN 1908.

UNTIL 1912. RICHARD BLAIR CONTINUED TO WORK IN INDIA, WITH ONLY BRIEF VISITS TO HIS FAMILY IN ENGLAND.

ERIC BLAIR THUS SELDOM SAW HIS FATHER UNTIL HE WAS EIGHT YEARS OLD, AND WAS THEN ENROLLED IN THE FIRST OF THREE BOARDING SCHOOLS, IN WHICH HE

REMAINED UNTIL THE END OF HIS CHILDHOOD. NOT SURPRISINGLY THEREFORE, ORWELL REPORTS THAT HE WAS NOT PARTICULARLY FOND OF HIS FATHER—SEEING HIM MAINLY AS A GRUFF OLDER MAN, 18 YEARS SENIOR TO ERIC'S MOTHER, WITH A ONE-WORD VOCABULARY:

Don't.

ERIC'S MOTHER WAS MUCH MORE CONGENIAL, A LIVELY WOMAN SYMPATHETIC TO THE WOMEN'S SUFFRAGE MOVEMENT AND REMEMBERED (BY ONE OF ORWELL'S CLASSMATES) AS

slightly exotic and gypsy-like.

ERIC VERY MUCH LOVED HIS MOTHER BUT DID NOT CONFIDE IN HER. HIS LIFE-LONG RETICENCE WAS EVIDENT FROM THE START.

TELL ME, ERIC!

ERIC'S BRIGHTNESS WAS ALSO APPARENT EARLY. BY THE TIME HE WAS EIGHT HIS PARENTS HOPED HE'D QUALIFY FOR

ONE OF THE BETTER RULING-CLASS SCHOOLS— HARROW, OR ETON.

THIS WAS A BOLD HOPE, SINCE ETON (FOR EXAMPLE) ACCEPTED ONLY THIRTEEN ACA- DEMICALLY ADVANCED NEW STUDENTS EACH YEAR.

TO THIS END, THE BLAIRS' ENROLLED ERIC IN AN ELITE ANGLICAN "PREPARATORY SCHOOL" IN 1911, ST. CYPRIAN'S:— WHERE, SAID CYRIL CONNOLLY (ERIC'S FRIEND AND LATER THE FOUNDER OF HORIZON) THE BOYS LEARNED

AS FAST AS FEAR COULD TEACH US!

ERIC'S EXPERIENCE AT ST. CYPRIAN'S WAS UNQUESTIONABLY THE WORST OF HIS CHILDHOOD AND BEST PUBLICIZED.

IT WAS NOT STRICTLY TYPICAL HOWEVER.

UNTIL EIGHT, ERIC LED A FAIRLY HAPPY LIFE, FEELING AWKWARD AND INADEQUATE

BUT NOT UN- LOVED.

AT THE AGE OF FOUR HE DICTATED HIS FIRST POEM. HE CREDITS A LINE ABOUT

...tigers with chair- like teeth...

TO THE INFLUENCE OF WILLIAM BLAKE.

BY AGE FIVE ERIC HAD DE- CIDED TO BE A WRITER— A SUBTERRANEAN PERSONAL DECISION HE NEVER COMPLETELY ABANDONED, EVEN IN BURMA. HE KNEW HE HAD

A FACILITY WITH WORDS AND A POWER OF FACING UNPLEASANT FACTS.

—A POWER WHICH PROVED USEFUL WHEN IT CAME TIME TO REFLECT UPON THE ST. CYPRIAN'S EXPERIENCE.

Learning to Conform

St. Cyprian's was an elite "preparatory school" designed to prepare ruling-class children for the so-called "public schools" (in reality, private boarding schools) so central to the English class hierarchy in 1911. It was already a cliché that England's battles were won, in advance, "on the playing fields of Eton."

Even more than the universities, the great public schools were the source of statesmen, military leaders, etc.

To qualify for such a school, Eric Blair and his peers first had to negotiate the hazards of a preparatory school. St. Cyprian's was a particularly aristocratic prep school, with an annual tuition of £180 (then a sky-high figure). This lordly tuition paid for the company of 100 fellow students in a school with two playing fields, two large residence halls, seven live-in "masters," a drill sergeant, and a matron.

Like most schools of its type, St. Cyprian's was for boys only. Its proprietors were Mr. and Mrs. Vaughn Wilkes.

"In effect there were three castes in the school. There was the minority with an aristocratic or millionaire background, there were the children of the ordinary suburban rich, who made up the bulk of the school, and there were a few underlings like myself."

unishment for "the underlings" (usually the less well-to-do) was inflicted regularly and sadistically for the slightest infringement of protocol. The St. Cyprian's proprietors were formidable disciplinarians. Headmaster Wilkes— "Sambo" to his terrified charges— frequently caned refractory pupils, kicked them on the shins, or rapped them with a silver pencil.

Mrs. Wilkes—"Flip"—was even stricter, with a fondness for hair pulling; she was clearly the primary force in the school, and several graduates referred to her as a veritable Queen Elizabeth, with a retinue of courtiers, aides, and supplicants.

The pressure was greatest on scholarship students, who were "crammed with learning as cynically as a goose is crammed for Christmas."

Mrs. Wilkes

The idea was to reflect honor on St. Cyprian's by having Eric and the few other underlings perform well on public school examinations. Eric's success would be a feather in the Vaughn Wilkes' cap, and would entice new pupils. The "Christmas goose," in other words, was expected to produce a golden egg.

Eric was not wholly cowed by the harsh discipline meted out at St. Cyprian's. A classmate, the noted photographer Cecil Beaton, regarded Eric's closest friend, Cyril Connolly, as "fascinating . . . so grown-up"; the sophisticated Connolly, meanwhile, was similarly impressed by Blair, recalling him as "born old," a "true rebel." Another classmate, Sir John Grotrian, remembers Eric boasting that his straight and butter-colored hair was "very well greased so that the teacher's fingers would slip off!"

Still, Eric was genuinely miserable at St. Cyprian's, and under the spell of his tormentors. "Round as a pudding was my face . . ." recalled Orwell later; adds Grotrian, "his face was moon shaped and all too often streaked with tears."

Eric felt great pressure to perform well scholastically. He felt outcast from his family and financially inferior to his classmates. Above all, Eric accepted the verdict of his "superiors"—that he was innately inferior, "deserving" of punishment, an ill-starred child menaced by jealous gods . . .

This is the point to remember if we wish to understand
Orwell's denunciation of St. Cyprian's in his posthumously
published memoir, "Such, Such Were the Joys" (completed
in May 1947, roughly when *1984* was started). Most critics
misconstrue this essay completely, seeing it simply as a
confessional tale of humiliation and self-loathing—or
(worse) as evidence of Orwell's "neurotic" antipathy to
authority.

With Orwell, radical ideas tend to be psychologized
out of existence. When this started to happen during
his lifetime—a critic conjectured that the police-
state of *1984* was merely the English prep school
writ large—Orwell replied ironically that only the
complacent English could view a country prep
school as the zenith of all political horrors. There are
terrors far worse . . .

Still, the prep school *does* have something in common with the police-state: in part, the psychology of
submissiveness which encourages underlings to feel,
often, that tyranny is proper and legitimate. The
problem is not why dogs bite the hand that feeds
them, but why they *lick* the hand that *beats* them.

Why do the oppressed frequently sanction
their own oppression? "Such, Such Were
the Joys" is a tentative answer. "Our chief
clue is that we were once children ourselves . . ."

Like Dickens, Orwell takes children as a particularly representative example of the maltreated. The miserable Eric of the later essay resembles many classic Dickens children: Sissy Jupe, abused by the nefarious McChokeumchild at Gradgrind's school; little David Copperfield, at the losing end of the lash . . .

"No one, at any rate no English writer, has written better about childhood than Dickens . . . I must have been about nine years old when I first read *David Copperfield*. The mental atmosphere of the opening chapters was so immediately intelligible to me that I vaguely imagined they had been written *by a child*."

Dickens portrayed cruelty in countless ways, in a mood of passionate indictment and sympathy. So did Orwell—who, said his friend Julian Symons, "always wrote from the point of view of a child."

Submission to unwise or unjust authority is a crucial issue for Orwell not only politically, but in terms of the personal experiences which led him to form his political views.

Viewing authority with implicit faith led Eric Blair from school to Burma, in accord with his father's wish—and into imperial service, in submission to the British Empire and its precepts. This faith in authority had its roots in Eric's childhood—a childhood which, like that of the hero of the popular children's book of the day, *Eric, or Little by Little*, revolved around the application and acceptance of tyrannical discipline.

One prerequisite for submissiveness is exposure to tyranny. This Eric experienced upon leaving home. "Your home might be far from perfect, but it was at least a place ruled by love rather than by fear."

Doubtless 'for his own good,' to 'give him a chance in life,' Eric's parents arranged his entry into St. Cyprian's. The blow was cruel and unforgettable.

"At eight years old you were suddenly taken out of this warm nest and flung into a world of force and fraud and secrecy, like a gold-fish into a tank full of pike. Against no matter what degree of bullying you had no redress."

The title of Orwell's essay was drawn from William Blake's "The Echoing Green." Blake had celebrated the family circle: "Such, such were the joys, When we all, girls and boys, In our youth time were seen, On the Echoing Green . . . The sun does descend, And our sports have an end. Round the laps of their mothers, Many sisters and brothers, Like birds in their nest, Are ready for rest . . ."

Eric's unhappy departure from the nest resulted from the economic insecurity of a "lower-upper-middle class" family eager to move up the class ladder. Eric's intelligence offered a chance to achieve precisely this . . .

The significance of Eric's chance to better himself was rubbed in on every occasion at St. Cyprian's.

"Very early it was impressed upon me that I had no chance of a decent future unless I won a scholarship at a public school. Either I won my scholarship, or I must leave school at fourteen and become, in Sambo's favorite phrase, 'a little office boy at forty pounds a year!' . . . It is not easy to convey to a grown-up person the sense of strain, of nerving oneself for some terrible, all-deciding combat, as the date of the examination crept nearer . . ."

Eric spent five years preparing for 2½ days of examinations—in Latin, Greek, history, science, mathematics, etc. The method of training was drilling, to facilitate memorization rather than understanding.

"I recall positive orgies of dates, with the keener boys leaping up and down in their eagerness to shout out the right answers, and at the same time not feeling the faintest interest in the mysterious events they were naming.
"1587?"
"Massacre of St. Bartholomew!"
"1707?"
"Death of Aurangzeeb!"
"1713?"
"Treaty of Utrecht!"

A dismal education, indeed!

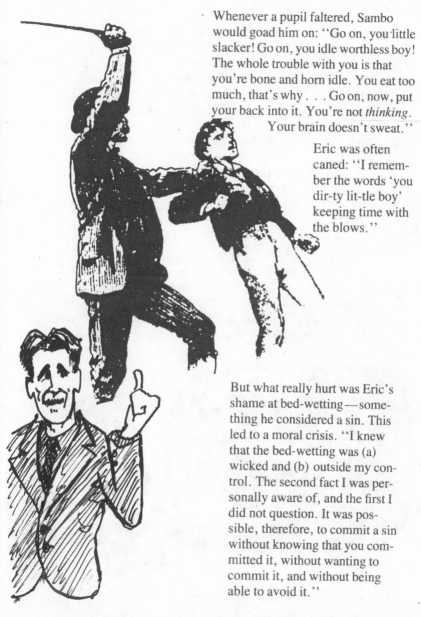

Whenever a pupil faltered, Sambo would goad him on: "Go on, you little slacker! Go on, you idle worthless boy! The whole trouble with you is that you're bone and horn idle. You eat too much, that's why . . . Go on, now, put your back into it. You're not *thinking*. Your brain doesn't sweat."

Eric was often caned: "I remember the words 'you dir-ty lit-tle boy' keeping time with the blows."

But what really hurt was Eric's shame at bed-wetting—something he considered a sin. This led to a moral crisis. "I knew that the bed-wetting was (a) wicked and (b) outside my control. The second fact I was personally aware of, and the first I did not question. It was possible, therefore, to commit a sin without knowing that you committed it, without wanting to commit it, and without being able to avoid it."

The conclusion? "Sin was not necessarily something that you did: it might be something that happened to you." And no effort of will could make Eric good.

Not that Eric didn't try to be good. "Night after night I prayed, with a fervor never previously attained in my prayers, 'Please God, do not let me wet my bed! Oh, please God, do not let me wet my bed!', but it made remarkably little difference."

An added fillip to Eric's moral dilemma came with the avid repression of sexuality at St. Cyprian's. Some sexual transgression had occurred (group masturbation?) and a climate of general accusation pervaded the school.

"Guilt seemed to hang in the air like a pall of smoke. A solemn, black-haired imbecile of an assistant master, who was later to be a Member of Parliament, took the older boys to a secluded room and delivered a talk on the Temple of the Body. 'Don't you realize what a wonderful thing your body is?' he asked gravely. 'You talk of your motor-car

engines, your Rolls-Royces and Daimlers and so on. Don't you understand that no engine ever made is fit to be compared with your body? And then you go and wreck it, ruin it—for life!' "

So it became clear that not only can one do wrong against one's will, "one can also do wrong without ever discovering what one has done or why it was wrong." Eric's moral crisis deepened.

Above all, Eric believed what he was told. "A child may be a mass of egoism and rebelliousness, but it has no accumulated experience to give it confidence in its own judgements. On the whole it will accept what it is told, and it will believe in the most fantastic way in the knowledge and powers of the adults surrounding it."

Even adults—the same children grown up—may know too little of the world to evolve critical faculties. Substitute the word "leaders" for "adults" in Orwell's last sentence, and one of the paramount problems of politics emerges—that tyrannized people very often *accept* the authority, judgement, and power of their "superiors." Napoleons and mini-Napoleons seem *legitimate*.

Why? To explore this, Orwell chose to scrutinize his memories— to recall submissiveness from the inside.

"I see now, of course, that from Sambo's point of view I was a good speculation. He sank money in me, and he looked to get it back in the form of prestige . . . But it is difficult for a child to realize that a school is primarily a commercial venture. Flip and Sambo had chosen to befriend me, and their friendship included canings, reproaches and humiliations, which were good for me and saved me from an office stool."

Eric arrived at an unquestioning conformism. "Very early, I reached the conclusion . . . that you were no good unless you had £100,000." Every desirable quality—"beauty, charm, athleticism, and something called 'guts' or 'character' which, in reality, meant the power to impose your will on others"—came packaged in money.

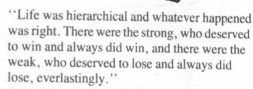

"Life was hierarchical and whatever happened was right. There were the strong, who deserved to win and always did win, and there were the weak, who deserved to lose and always did lose, everlastingly."

Still, "subjective conformity" proved impossible for Eric. The rules were so constructed that he was bound to break them—and be punished, everlastingly.

Eric found similar problems in religion. He knew, for example, that he was supposed to love God, but also fear him. This seemed psychologically surreal. "How could you love someone whom you feared?" Deep down, Eric knew that he feared God—and *hated* him.

The same applied to Flip and Sambo. But Eric was ashamed of his hatred and afraid to express it. Also, cravenly, he wanted to curry favor with his oppressors.

"Whenever one had the chance to suck up, one *did* suck up, and at the first smile one's hatred turned into a sort of cringing love."

Feeling morally bound to love the people who bound him physically, Eric hated himself—for hating *them*. Even his subjective resistance thus worked against him: it is a sin to resist abuse from your betters; the oppressor who castigates you for your inborn sinfulness deserves your thanks.

"I did not see that the weak have the right to make a different set of rules for themselves."

Thus Eric Blair learned to conform. The outlook which prompted his service to the Empire in Burma was formed when Eric *accepted* being crammed like a Christmas goose to escape office drudgery.

Eric Blair accepted his class destiny—which meant accepting the class system *per se*. He reconciled himself not only to experiencing tyranny, but to practicing it.

Class conformism became the principal subject of Orwell's mature art. Can conformity be broken? This was the focal question at the heart of every one of Orwell's books, and most of his key essays.

Orwell is sometimes accused of jeering at people who conform, as an aristocratic outsider who could afford to cultivate his eccentricities. The truth is quite different. In fact, Orwell stoically conformed to a Spartan regimen (in school, and Burma) for long years.

His best insights into conformism derive from his own early conformism. And Orwell did not ''jeer'' at those who failed to break from stifling routines—he *empathized*, and tried to break free himself.

The risks of Orwell's later nonconformism were substantial.

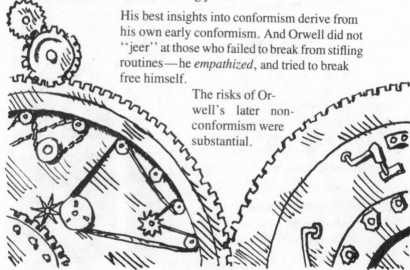

To say nothing of his later war experience in Spain, Orwell exchanged a safe career (and family approval) for a forlorn, implausible, solitary effort to write. Much of the poverty he supposedly "invited," for voyeuristic reasons, was in fact unavoidable for a struggling writer. And there were few alternatives, once the imperial tie had been cut. Orwell was *not* a university graduate. He did *not* have fortunate family ties. To finance his writing, Orwell worked as precisely the equivalent of "a little office boy making forty pounds a year" from 1932–1936.

This does not make Orwell a "prole"—but it does shed light on the Scylla and Charybdis between which Eric Blair sailed on his voyage of self-discovery. You can be either a drudge— "shabby-genteel," an underling—or an imperial civil servant, a miniature boss: this was the choice Blair faced.

At first, he took the "lesser evil," winding up in Burma as a mini-boss. But later, Orwell realized that the very equation can be redefined—that the meager "gentility" of the writer, the political figure, has rewards beyond the usual class horizon. So Orwell took an independent path, transgressing his class limits by identifying with the exploited. He became "Orwell."

Capable of this metamorphosis by virtue of his background and education, Orwell urged an end to submissiveness for drudges everywhere. For most people, this requires not just personal resolve, but cooperative action. This too Orwell promoted.

Meanwhile, Eric Blair's youth was not all thorns. A few roses were strewn about.

Eric became an avid reader at about five, when he entered a day school called Sunnylands run by Anglican nuns. Other favorite childhood books included *Gulliver's Travels*, *Tom Sawyer*, *Rebecca of Sunnybrook Farm*, and *Coral Island*.

Cyril Connolly was Eric's first co-thinker. Together, they withstood St. Cyprian's, keeping alive a shared passion for literature.

Eric's closest non-school friends were the Buddicom children. Twelve-year-old Eric first met Jacintha, Prosper, and Guinever Buddicom in a style worthy of Lewis Carroll's Alice: on a family holiday, standing on his head.

Reports Jacintha Buddicom: "This was a feat we had never observed before, and we found it intriguing; so one of us, polite but curious, asked him 'Why are you standing on your head?' To which he replied: 'You are noticed more if you stand on your head than if you are right way up.' "

from E.B.

Eric, sister Avril, and the Buddicoms became fast friends, spending most holidays together for seven years. According to Jacintha's memoirs, and echoed by Avril Blair, croquet, bicycle polo, and cards were enjoyed by all. With Prosper and Guinever Buddicom, Eric "played tennis and went shooting."

With Jacintha, Eric developed an intellectual camaraderie which deepened into profound friendship. Jacintha and Eric talked books and wrote poetry. Eric wrote comic *vers d'occasion* "in imitation of Aristophanes," and revelled not only in Shakespeare, but in writing and reciting mock Shakespearean plays. Eric often told Jacintha that he planned to be a FAMOUS AUTHOR; they debated whether his collected works should be gilt-edged or not.

Jacintha later recalled Orwell as "the most interesting, the best informed, the kindest, the *nicest*" of the boys she knew.

In strange contrast to Eric Blair's feeling of internal exile at St. Cyprian's was the manner of his graduation—as a "conquering hero," accepted to Eton (which he attended from 1917 until 1921).

Eton's celebrated "playing fields" were much more comfortable for Eric than prep school had been. He entered King's College, an academic enclave of fewer than 70 students surrounded by a population of 900 so-called Oppidans (non-scholarship students). Later, Orwell applauded the "tolerant and civilized atmosphere" of the school. Though a fairly Byzantine maze of snobbish and educational distinctions, Eric adapted in his customary way: blithely conforming to the hierarchy and becoming "an odious little snob, but no worse than the other boys."

Eric slacked off so much in his studies that *60 years later* his tutor, Andrew Gow, still remembered him bitterly. Orwell ultimately placed 12th out of the 13 members of his 1921 King's College class. His brain was clearly not sweating as it might have been.

His feet, however, were still growing impressively. Eric was nearly 6'3" by graduation. He became so physically formidable that he won athletic colors for prowess at the medieval Wall Game.

A.S.F. Gow—his tutor at Eton.

Aldous Huxley taught Orwell French.

Continuing to write stories, comic verse, etc., Eric was on good but not intimate terms with his classmates. He affected an insouciance of manner and a bluntness of speech which never altogether vanished.

For a brief time he took French classes from the young Aldous Huxley.

In class terms Eric was still odd man out. Though the shabby-genteel Blair family had succeeded in placing their only son in august Etonian company, they did not plan to have him stay with this group. His path was to diverge—to India, where "the ambitious middle-class" could find a special niche. An Indian civil servant was the nearest thing to a moneyed aristocrat outside England, with servants, respectable pay, and prestige.

George Wansborough, a King's College classmate (and later a Bank of England Director), recalls Eric as "obviously a very different type of boy . . ." At graduation time, Eric was the only one of the 14 graduating scholarship students to leave England. Eleven went either to Oxford or Cambridge, and two went into family businesses.

The decision to leave Eton for South Asia must have been fairly unusual. An Eton administrator, John Crace, supplied Eric a bland character reference saying, with a trace of sarcasm, that he had never previously supplied a reference to the police.

Eric's genteel poverty led him to a unique post-Eton terminus: Burma. He conformed to his family's wishes . . .

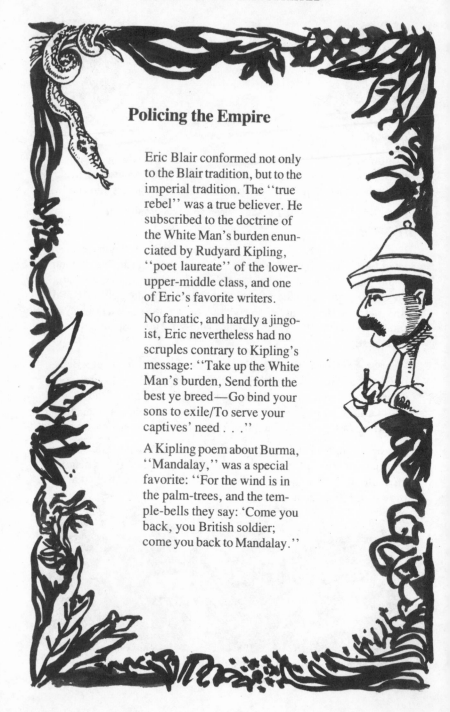

Policing the Empire

Eric Blair conformed not only to the Blair tradition, but to the imperial tradition. The "true rebel" was a true believer. He subscribed to the doctrine of the White Man's burden enunciated by Rudyard Kipling, "poet laureate" of the lower-upper-middle class, and one of Eric's favorite writers.

No fanatic, and hardly a jingo-ist, Eric nevertheless had no scruples contrary to Kipling's message: "Take up the White Man's burden, Send forth the best ye breed—Go bind your sons to exile/To serve your captives' need . . ."

A Kipling poem about Burma, "Mandalay," was a special favorite: "For the wind is in the palm-trees, and the temple-bells they say: 'Come you back, you British soldier; come you back to Mandalay.''

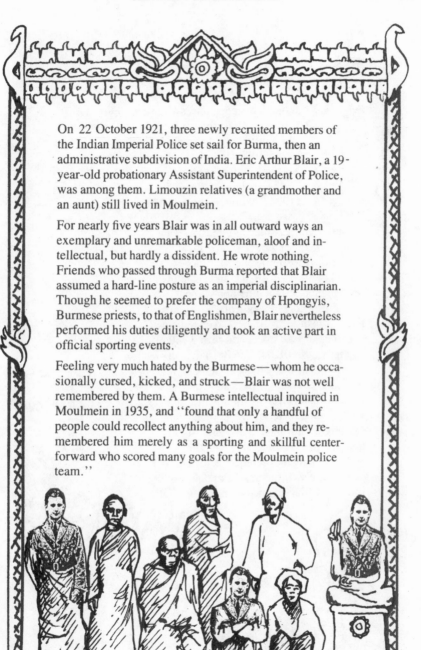

On 22 October 1921, three newly recruited members of the Indian Imperial Police set sail for Burma, then an administrative subdivision of India. Eric Arthur Blair, a 19-year-old probationary Assistant Superintendent of Police, was among them. Limouzin relatives (a grandmother and an aunt) still lived in Moulmein.

For nearly five years Blair was in all outward ways an exemplary and unremarkable policeman, aloof and intellectual, but hardly a dissident. He wrote nothing. Friends who passed through Burma reported that Blair assumed a hard-line posture as an imperial disciplinarian. Though he seemed to prefer the company of Hpongyis, Burmese priests, to that of Englishmen, Blair nevertheless performed his duties diligently and took an active part in official sporting events.

Feeling very much hated by the Burmese—whom he occasionally cursed, kicked, and struck—Blair was not well remembered by them. A Burmese intellectual inquired in Moulmein in 1935, and "found that only a handful of people could recollect anything about him, and they remembered him merely as a sporting and skillful center-forward who scored many goals for the Moulmein police team."

ll outward appearances to the contrary, however, Blair changed greatly in Burma. Ultimately, he found it impossible to repress either his developing hatred for the Empire, or his wish to write. His second book, *Burmese Days* (1934), expressed both feelings.

Orwell's Burmese metamorphosis did not happen in a vacuum. Several critical events of British rule over Burma occurred in the early 1920s, and an air of ferment and distant rebellion was palpable (especially to someone with antennae as sensitive as Blair's). And remember, the Far East in general stirred with change in the 1920s. The Bolshevik uprising was still very fresh in memory, and the Bolshevik regime was an active presence in Asian affairs—fighting for its spiritual and material life, perhaps, but fighting. Lenin and the Communist International paid considerable attention to Asia—seeing the prerequisite for a hurricane in the swirling misery of colonized Indians, Chinese, and others.

According to Orwell, "the real turning point in modern Burmese history [was] the annexation of Upper Burma in 1885," the result of the third Anglo-Burmese war. (Previous wars had been fought in 1824–26 and 1852.) Now, the whole of Burma—Upper and Lower—belonged to the British.

Although the Burmese had known something about the British Empire since an envoy of the East India Company first kneeled to the Burmese king in 1752, still, as late as 1820, the Burmese had enjoyed an independence and naive optimism made possible by geographic isolation. "It is curious to reflect that in 1820, or thereabouts, a Burmese army was sent to invade India, with orders to bring back the English Governor-General in chains, and, if necessary, to march on and capture London." Fleeting, blissful ignorance!

After the 1885 defeat, simmering resistance percolated just below the surface of Burmese society. Periodic small rebellions—villagers with pitchforks, nationalists leading demonstrations—were effectively put down. Sir Herbert White, former Lieutenant-Governor, expressed the prevailing colonial English sentiment in 1913 when he declared it "pernicious cant" to say that "our mission in Burma is the political education of the masses;" the British role, rather, is to bring "law and order to parts of barbary and to maintain them there."

However, the Burmese proved irrepressible. To start, they felt humiliated by the English decision to make Burma a province of India. When the English government compounded the problem in 1919 by granting India limited "dyarchy"—participation in government—without extending this to the Burmese, mass protests flared up. The Empire rectified its error in 1923 by allowing the Burmese limited dyarchy, too, but the damage was done.

Nationalist sentiments filtered into many different sectors of Burmese society, and dissent typified the 1920s.

Blair thus defended law and order in "barbary" at a very uncomfortable moment.

Fears of sedition were epidemic among Blair's fellow English, and the Burmese were less enchanted with their colonial oppressors than ever.

Little wonder, then, that Blair felt hated by the public. More remarkable is that he later came to *share* the Burmese hatred for the British Empire.

When Blair finally decided to leave Burma, two issues concerned him most. Both fall under the rubric "imperialism"—the exploitation of the Burmese, and the spiritual corruption of the English exploiters. In a 1946 letter to a conservative expert on Burma, F. Tennyson Jesse, Orwell summarized both objections: "In your book you said nothing about our economic exploitation of the country, the way in which, for instance, we get oil and other raw materials at a fraction of what they would cost if Burma were an independent country, and though you did mention it, you soft-pedalled the social misbehavior of the British . . .''

Blair's first public commentary on the English in Burma was an article in a small French radical journal, *Le Progrès civique* (4 May 1929). This was one of Blair's first published articles on any subject. Not yet a socialist, Blair was nevertheless clear in his perception of imperialism:

"One does not have to live in Burma long to see that Britain is complete master of the country. The Burmese, like some of the Indian provinces, have a parliament — always the show of demo-cracy — but this parliament in reality does not have any power."

(continued on page 54)

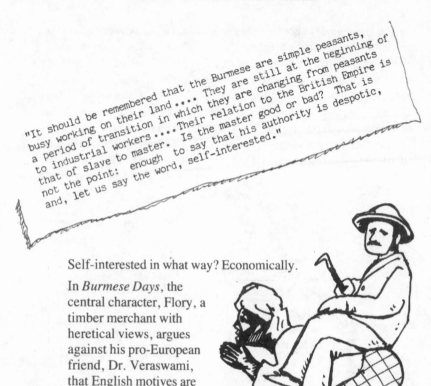

"It should be remembered that the Burmese are simple peasants, busy working on their land .... They are still at the beginning of a period of transition in which they are changing from peasants to industrial workers .... Their relation to the British Empire is that of slave to master. Is the master good or bad? That is not the point: enough to say that his authority is despotic, and, let us say the word, self-interested."

Self-interested in what way? Economically.

In *Burmese Days*, the central character, Flory, a timber merchant with heretical views, argues against his pro-European friend, Dr. Veraswami, that English motives are selfish.

''My dear doctor, how can you make out that we are in this country for any purpose except to steal? It's so simple. The official holds the Burman down while the business man goes through his pockets. Do you suppose my firm, for instance, could get its timber contracts if the country weren't in the hands of the British? Or the other timber firms, or the oil companies, or the miners and planters and traders? The British Empire is simply a device for giving trade monopolies to the English . . .''

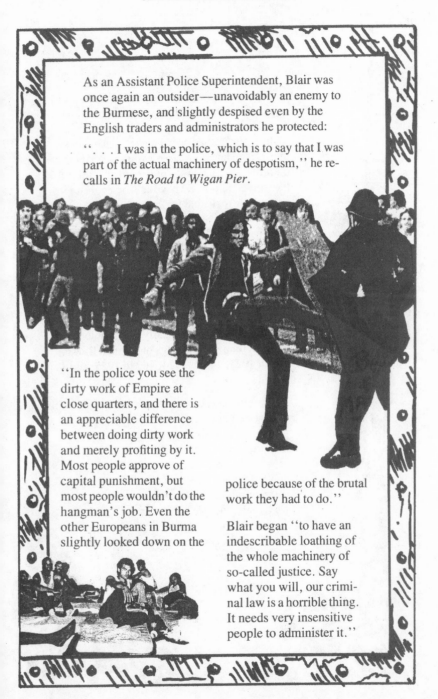

As an Assistant Police Superintendent, Blair was once again an outsider—unavoidably an enemy to the Burmese, and slightly despised even by the English traders and administrators he protected:

". . . I was in the police, which is to say that I was part of the actual machinery of despotism," he recalls in *The Road to Wigan Pier*.

"In the police you see the dirty work of Empire at close quarters, and there is an appreciable difference between doing dirty work and merely profiting by it. Most people approve of capital punishment, but most people wouldn't do the hangman's job. Even the other Europeans in Burma slightly looked down on the police because of the brutal work they had to do."

Blair began "to have an indescribable loathing of the whole machinery of so-called justice. Say what you will, our criminal law is a horrible thing. It needs very insensitive people to administer it."

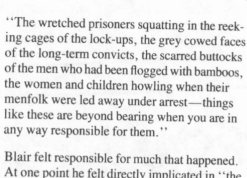

"The wretched prisoners squatting in the reeking cages of the lock-ups, the grey cowed faces of the long-term convicts, the scarred buttocks of the men who had been flogged with bamboos, the women and children howling when their menfolk were led away under arrest—things like these are beyond bearing when you are in any way responsible for them."

Blair felt responsible for much that happened. At one point he felt directly implicated in "the hangman's job":

"I watched a man hanged once; it seemed to me worse than a thousand murders."

Dating this hanging is nearly impossible since there were many hangings in colonial Burma: 116 in 1923, 145 in 1924, 162 in 1925, and 191 in 1927.

"I should expect to find that even in England many policemen, judges, prison warders, and the like are haunted by a secret horror of what they do. But in Burma it was a double oppression that we were committing. Not only were we hanging people and putting them in jail and so forth; we were doing it in the capacity of unwanted foreign invaders."

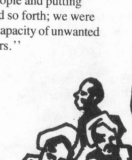

So this is what it meant to be among the ''shock absorbers of the bourgeoisie'' (the business class) at the border of the British Empire: forced to enforce alien laws to promote English profits, yet scorned for the effort, even by the English. Evidently, it is not quite genteel to have blood on your boots. And few of the victims find it admirable, either.

Not surprisingly, the sensitive Blair felt a massive loss of self-respect in Burma. Consider his dilemma: feared by the Burmese people, whom he liked; increasingly bitter about his callous fellow Englishmen; guilt-ridden; yet forced to accept the bitter pill of silence to keep his job.

Blair felt especially guilty for protecting his job with hypocritical silence. But with no clear alternative, what else could he do? He bit his tongue.

''There is no freedom of speech, and merely to be overheard making a seditious remark may damage one's career. All over India there are Englishmen who secretly loathe the system of which they are part; and just occasionally, when they are certain of being in the right company, their hidden bitterness overflows.''

''The real bourgeoisie . . . have their money as a thick layer of padding between themselves and the class they plunder.'' Not so the shock-absorbers. Ultimately, Eric Blair was shocked into rebellion. *Burmese Days* stunningly evokes both his experience and the dissent it produced.

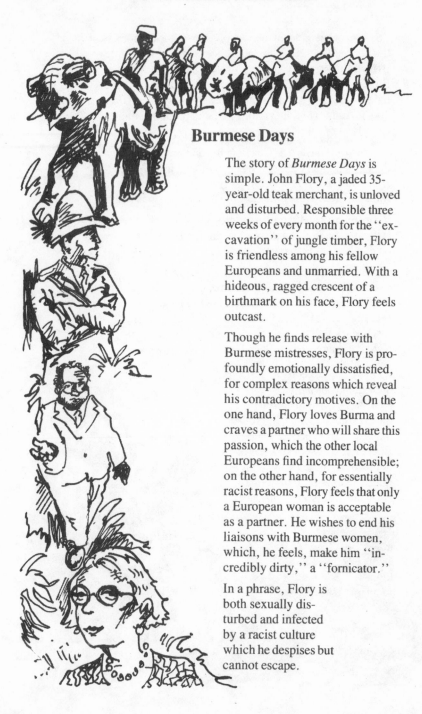

Burmese Days

The story of *Burmese Days* is simple. John Flory, a jaded 35-year-old teak merchant, is unloved and disturbed. Responsible three weeks of every month for the "excavation" of jungle timber, Flory is friendless among his fellow Europeans and unmarried. With a hideous, ragged crescent of a birthmark on his face, Flory feels outcast.

Though he finds release with Burmese mistresses, Flory is profoundly emotionally dissatisfied, for complex reasons which reveal his contradictory motives. On the one hand, Flory loves Burma and craves a partner who will share this passion, which the other local Europeans find incomprehensible; on the other hand, for essentially racist reasons, Flory feels that only a European woman is acceptable as a partner. He wishes to end his liaisons with Burmese women, which, he feels, make him "incredibly dirty," a "fornicator."

In a phrase, Flory is both sexually disturbed and infected by a racist culture which he despises but cannot escape.

All Flory's inner tensions are forced to the surface by the suffocating pettiness and racism of the small European enclave to which he belongs in Kyauktada (a town of 4000, just seven of whom are Europeans: three timber merchants, a merchant's wife, a forestry official, a police superintendent, and a central administrator). Situations arise which demand courage from Flory, and he fails pathetically. He befriends an Indian doctor in need of help which Flory could easily provide—a word at the European Club would solve the problem. Yet Flory is unable to stand up to the racist vituperation this would invite. He feels weak and contemptible.

Into this drama walks pretty, unsuspecting Elizabeth Lackersteen, niece of a timber merchant and fresh from Paris: twenty-two, with fashionably short blonde hair and tortoise shell glasses.

Desperate for proper, respectable European love, Flory courts Elizabeth with eagerness and ox-like stupidity.

Lost in romantic fantasy, Flory imagines Elizabeth to be the sensitive non-racist he so much desires.

Elizabeth, it turns out —though Flory is unwilling to see—is ultra-conventional: frightened and repelled by the Burmese, attracted to courage and violence, repulsed by ''braininess'' and ideas. Flory's courtship is hopeless, but he's too blind to understand.

He breaks with Ma Hla May, his pretty, scheming Burmese concubine, and pursues Elizabeth. She too hopes for marriage, and manages, at moments, to mistake Flory for a proper *pukka sahib*. Far less desperate than Flory, however, Elizabeth is rudely reminded time after time that Flory actually *likes* the Burmese, and cherishes his ''brainy'' heresies.

Flory loses Elizabeth briefly to an upper-class snob, all looks and *hauteur* and horsemanship. Shattered, he waits. His rival leaves. Flory then rises to unexpected courage.

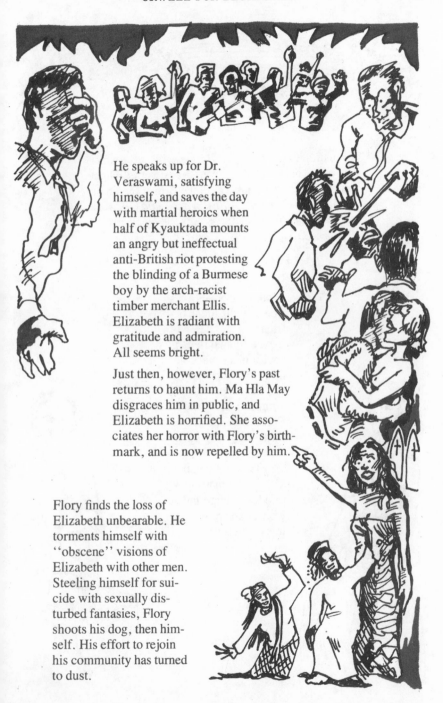

He speaks up for Dr. Veraswami, satisfying himself, and saves the day with martial heroics when half of Kyauktada mounts an angry but ineffectual anti-British riot protesting the blinding of a Burmese boy by the arch-racist timber merchant Ellis. Elizabeth is radiant with gratitude and admiration. All seems bright.

Just then, however, Flory's past returns to haunt him. Ma Hla May disgraces him in public, and Elizabeth is horrified. She associates her horror with Flory's birthmark, and is now repelled by him.

Flory finds the loss of Elizabeth unbearable. He torments himself with ''obscene'' visions of Elizabeth with other men. Steeling himself for suicide with sexually disturbed fantasies, Flory shoots his dog, then himself. His effort to rejoin his community has turned to dust.

Claustrophobic and bitter, *Burmese Days* is a striking book, one of the few novels to cast a critical light on the follies and injustices of the British Empire in India. E. M. Forster's *A Passage to India* (1924) is the only clearly comparable work, and it clearly influenced Orwell's outlook.

Each book posits a dissident Englishman befriending and defending a besieged Indian doctor in a small colonial city, where all social life revolves around an all-white European Club and a tiny group of English officials. In both books the plot hinges on the arrival of a marriage-minded young Englishwoman and ensuing misadventures.

The temper of the two books, however, could hardly be more at variance. Forster wrote in a mild, ironic, philosophizing mood, concerned above all to probe the vast gulf between Indian and English mentalities. His reproach to imperialism is benign and qualified. His characters are seriocomic, and even his most debased characters are capable of a debased nobility. He offers a panoramic picture, with numerous thinly drawn characters, semi-mystic musings, and a highly embroidered plot.

Burmese Days, by contrast, is stark. Orwell's characters are stern, brutal, foolish, weak. His vision is narrow and ruthless, the antithesis of Forster's cheerful ambivalence, and his interest is personal psychology.

Where Forster's book resembles a broad-minded academic treatise, *Burmese Days* resembles an expressionist play— with a small number of sets, minimal action, and ruinous obsessions leading to a violent climax.

Where Orwell and Forster most significantly *agree* is in their picture of the colonial experience. . . .

The English, said Forster, "circulate like an ice stream" through India and the Dominions. Memorable portraits from this colonial ice-stream are drawn by both writers...

Forster's

"I am out here to work, mind, to hold this wretched country by force... most of the Indians you see are seditious... incident after incident, all due to propaganda... my personal opinion is, it's the Jews..."

HEASLOP THE MAGISTRATE, THE "RED-NOSED BOY"

"The worst thing in my whole career has happened. Miss Quested has been insulted in one of the Marabar Caves."

TURTON THE COLLECTOR, THE PROVINCIAL DIRECTOR, WANTED TO FLOG EVERY NATIVE THAT HE SAW

Orwell's

"Always the same story with these rebellions—peter out almost before they've begun. Would you believe it, I've never fired my gun at a fellow yet... eleven years of it and never killed a man. Depressing."

WESTFIELD, DEPUTY SUPERINTENDENT OF POLICE, DISPIRITED

Urrrpp...!

MR. LACKERSTEEN, BLUFF, BEEFY 40-YEAR OLD MANAGER OF A LOCAL TIMBER COMPANY

Deputy Commissioner Macgregor, bespectacled 60-year old, "stiffened at the word 'nigger', which is discountenanced in India. Provided they were given no freedom he thought them the most charming people alive."

The five pukka sahib precepts: Keep up our Prestige · The Firm Hand (without the velvet glove) · We White Men

"IT'S NOT THE TIME FOR SITTING DOWN. IT'S TIME FOR ACTION. CALL IN THE TROOPS AND CLEAR THE BAZAARS... NOTHING'S TOO BAD FOR THESE PEOPLE."

"AT LAST SOME SENSE IS BEING TALKED!"

MRS. TURTON

MAJOR CALLENDAR, THE CIVIL SURGEON, BREAKING INTO A ROAR

"THEY KILLED A WHITE MAN! OH, THE SWINE, THE SWINE, HOW THEY OUGHT TO SUFFER FOR IT! WHY DID WE MAKE THESE CURSED KID-GLOVE LAWS? WHY DO WE TAKE EVERYTHING LYING DOWN? JUST SUPPOSE THIS HAD HAPPENED IN A GERMAN COLONY, BEFORE THE WAR! THE GOOD OLD GERMANS! THEY KNEW HOW TO TREAT THE NIGGERS. REPRISALS! RHINOCEROS HIDE WHIPS! RAID THEIR VILLAGES, KILL THEIR CATTLE, BURN THEIR CROPS..."

ELLIS, SMALL AND SHARP FEATURED TIMBER MANAGER

"REALLY. I THINK THE LAZINESS OF THESE SERVANTS IS GETTING TOO SHOCKING. DON'T YOU AGREE, MR. MACGREGOR? WE SEEM TO HAVE NO AUTHORITY OVER THE NATIVES NOWADAYS, WITH ALL THESE DREADFUL REFORMS, THE INSOLENCE THEY LEARN FROM THE NEWSPAPERS. IN SOME WAYS THEY ARE GETTING ALMOST AS BAD AS THE LOWER CLASSES AT HOME."

"OH, HARDLY AS BAD AS THAT, I TRUST. STILL, I AM AFRAID THAT THERE IS NO DOUBT THAT THE DEMOCRATIC SPIRIT IS CREEPING IN, EVEN HERE."

MRS. LACKERSTEEN

ESPRIT DE CORPS. A MILE.

MUST HANG TOGETHER. GIVE THEM AN INCH AND THEY'LL TAKE

Against the background of this portrayal of colonial small-mindedness and bigotry, Orwell communicates his central message—that partial, incoherent resistance to a large evil invites personal tragedy.

Flory had arrived in Burma in 1914, and had fallen victim to the temptations of colonial life. Corrupted spiritually by the comparative wealth, social superiority, and insularity that the English enjoyed in Burma, Flory abused his privileges. He took to drink and loveless relations with Burmese women. He was curt and short-tempered with servants and timber workers. His hunger for spiritual communion with his equals rose, but in inverse proportion to his ability to cultivate such communion.

Where, previously, Flory's birthmark had distinguished him, Flory was now marked by his inability to build friendships—and by his unwillingness to blend in with his fellow empire-builders.

Dissolute and weakening though he was, Flory retained just enough critical insight and courage to renounce his imperial patrimony.

"What was at the center of all his thoughts now, and what poisoned everything, was the ever bitterer hatred of the atmosphere of imperialism in which he lived. For as his brain developed—you cannot stop your brain developing, and it is one of the tragedies of the half-educated that they develop late, when they are already committed to some wrong way of life—he had grasped the truth about the English and their Empire."

Flory could neither break with the Empire decisively nor parrot the malignant nonsense of his fellow colonizers. A late-blooming rebel, Flory was "already committed to a wrong way of life" and unable to wrench free.

In conversation with Veraswami he would momentarily dissent: "Such a glorious holiday from *them . . .* from my fellow Empire-builders. British prestige, the white man's burden, the pukka sahib *sans peur et sans reproche*—you know. Such a relief to be out of the stink of it for a while."

For his views, Flory was naturally reviled by his compatriots (even though he tried hard to give no offense). "Downright Bolshevism, damnit!" splutters Mr. Lackersteen. The other Europeans agree. To Elizabeth, Flory appears perverse, strangely attached to "these *disgusting* people."

He is "her deadliest word—a highbrow, to be classed with Lenin . . ."

Flory was afflicted with what Forster called "this evil of brains"—a curse in a tight-knit colonial community where unthinking racial solidarity is *de rigueur*.

Forster: "The man who doesn't toe the line is lost."

Flory didn't toe the line.

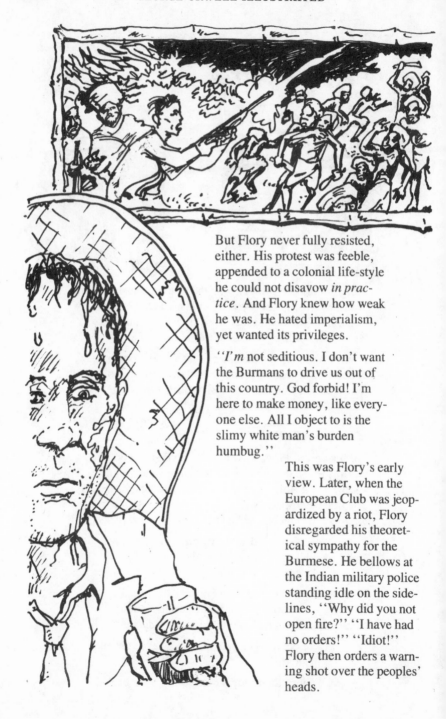

But Flory never fully resisted, either. His protest was feeble, appended to a colonial life-style he could not disavow *in practice*. And Flory knew how weak he was. He hated imperialism, yet wanted its privileges.

"I'm not seditious. I don't want the Burmans to drive us out of this country. God forbid! I'm here to make money, like everyone else. All I object to is the slimy white man's burden humbug."

This was Flory's early view. Later, when the European Club was jeopardized by a riot, Flory disregarded his theoretical sympathy for the Burmese. He bellows at the Indian military police standing idle on the sidelines, "Why did you not open fire?" "I have had no orders!" "Idiot!" Flory then orders a warning shot over the peoples' heads.

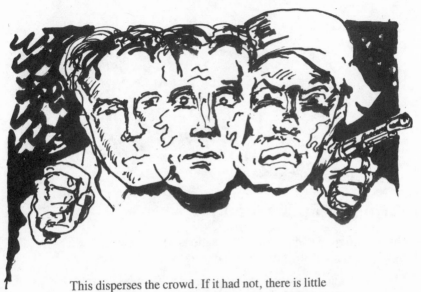

This disperses the crowd. If it had not, there is little doubt that Flory would have ordered a slaughter.

Even Fielding, Flory's vastly calmer, more resourceful counterpart in *A Passage To India,* reverts, in the end, to a complacent accommodation with the Empire. But where Fielding shifts comfortably, almost imperceptibly from heroic minor resistance to untroubled acquiescence, Flory falls apart.

Flory's fall is the result of his transgressions among the Burmese—whom he has failed to embrace *warmly enough* for a real break from injustice. His half-hearted, ''half-educated'' rebellion brings him only woe. It proves to be too little and too late to redeem him.

Either resist effectively, or do not resist at all. This is Orwell's implicit message upon leaving Burma.

Writing, Eileen, Socialism

Burma, no right to dominate other nations. He would
have ended the British Raj then and there.''

Despite this anti-imperialism, however, Eric Blair broke from
the police for essentially private rather than political reasons.
He refused service to imperialism not to *oppose* imperialism,
but for personal freedom—to write. ''I wanted to write enormous naturalistic novels with unhappy endings,'' he later said;
if these novels chanced to have political meaning, fine; but
Orwell's goal was self-expression.

There are four reasons for writing, Orwell
said: ''Sheer egoism, aesthetic enthusiasm,
historical impulse, and political purpose.''

Initially, egoism and enthusiasm were Orwell's primary
motives; the quality of his earliest prose, however, did not
give much reason for enthusiasm.

Says Ruth Pitter: ''He was like
a cow with a musket. . . . We
tried not to be discouraging,
but we used to laugh till we
cried at some of the bits he
showed us. . . .''

Before long, though, Orwell's writing improved dramatically. This change in the caliber of his writing coincided with the early stages of his shift from egoism to political purpose. Evident, roughly, from 1929–30, this shift was essentially complete by 1936.

"Every line of serious work that I have written since 1936 has been written directly or indirectly, *against* totalitarianism and *for* democratic Socialism. . . ." To understand the transition that made Eric Blair a political writer, it is necessary to follow the tangled path of his engagement with poverty, the poor, and the proletariat. These were his principal early subjects.

"I now realized that there was no need to go as far as Burma to find tyranny and exploitation. Here in England, down under one's feet, were the submerged working class. . . ."

Orwell made forays into the impoverished East End of London in ragged clothes. Remember, this was an era of great interest in the poor. Charlie Chaplin's "little tramp" was the premiere attraction in the movie world; Orwell became their premiere chronicler.

Living on his savings, Orwell tried to become a professional writer. "I did just about as well as do most young people who take up a literary career—that is to say, not at all. In the spring of 1928 I set off for Paris to live cheaply while writing two novels—which I regret to say were never published."

For a year and a half Eric lived on the Left Bank near his aunt, Nellie Adam, and gave English lessons. His neighborhood was a colorful, raucous slum.

When he was robbed in late 1929, Orwell took work as a *plongeur* (a kitchen worker in a hotel) for two months. He published a *Le Monde* article, his *Progrès civique* article on Burma, and a brief essay for *G.K.'s Weekly* in England.

Back in England in 1930, Orwell eked out a marginal existence with family help.

Writing incessantly—described by his old friend Richard Rees as "absorbed, obsessed"—Orwell also enjoyed his first success. Several polished book reviews in respected magazines preceded the January 1933, publication of *Down and Out in Paris and London,* which won critical praise and briefly became a best seller.

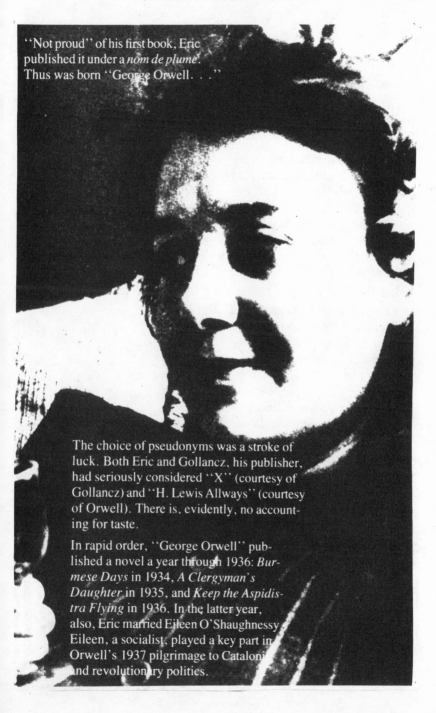

"Not proud" of his first book, Eric published it under a *nom de plume*. Thus was born "George Orwell. . ."

The choice of pseudonyms was a stroke of luck. Both Eric and Gollancz, his publisher, had seriously considered "X" (courtesy of Gollancz) and "H. Lewis Allways" (courtesy of Orwell). There is, evidently, no accounting for taste.

In rapid order, "George Orwell" published a novel a year through 1936: *Burmese Days* in 1934, *A Clergyman's Daughter* in 1935, and *Keep the Aspidistra Flying* in 1936. In the latter year, also, Eric married Eileen O'Shaughnessy. Eileen, a socialist, played a key part in Orwell's 1937 pilgrimage to Catalonia and revolutionary politics.

''The nicest person I have met for a long time.'' This was
Orwell's initial reaction upon meeting Eileen. Until her tragic
death in 1945, they were very happy.

Though a successful novelist, Orwell was still penni-
less in 1936. He had kept himself afloat working odd
jobs: as a tutor, a private-school teacher, and (in
1934–35) as a part-time bookstore clerk.

Teaching intrigued Orwell, and he took it seriously.
''No job is more fascinating than teaching if you have
a free hand at it—though if you are forced to bore your
pupils and oppress them, they will hate you for it.''
The best moments in teaching are ''. . . the times
when the children's enthusiasm leaps up, like an answering flame, to meet your own.'' Orwell was well-
liked as a teacher, though something of a disciplinarian.

Eileen's career had been equally checkered.
From an Anglo-Irish family slightly better off
than the Blairs, Eileen was twenty-two when
she received an English honors degree from
Oxford in 1927. Since then she had worked,
alternately, as a typist, a journalist, a teacher,
and as companion to elderly Dame Cadbury
of the chocolate-making family. When Eileen
met Orwell, she was an M.A. psychology
student.

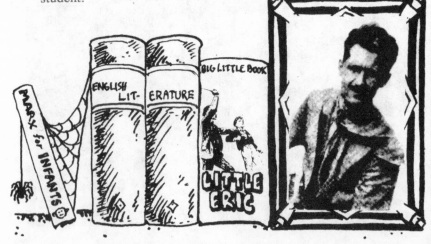

Considering how many of his friends were socialists, Orwell's passage to socialism was surprisingly slow. He proved to be anything but glib about his commitments.

Is socialism possible? After years of wrestling with this basic question, Orwell finally decided 'yes' in 1936. He had rejected this conclusion many times previously. For years Richard Rees had tried to persuade Orwell to substitute socialism for ''Tory anarchism.'' Many others had made similar efforts, *e.g.,* Mabel Fierz, who promoted *Down and Out,* and Nellie Adam (Orwell's aunt), a leader of the Workers' Esperanto Association of the World.

Victor Gollancz, Orwell's publisher, was a Communist. Orwell's bookstore employers, Francis and Myfanwy Westrope, belonged to the left-socialist Independent Labour Party (ILP). Reg Groves, a founder of British Trotskyism, was Orwell's immediate predecessor in the bookstore. Orwell's co-worker was Jon Kimche, later editor of the socialist newspaper *Tribune.* And the owner of Orwell's London flat, Rosalind Obermeyer, was a leftish Jungian psychologist who introduced Orwell to Eileen.

Orwell showed familiarity with radicalism in his writings, too. The 1928–29 articles from Paris were definitely red-tinged—attacking journalists as ''publicity agents for big business,'' defending censorship victims (Joyce, Lawrence), etc.

A typical passage in the London section of *Down and Out* is Orwell's encounter with the disabled sidewalk artist, Bozo, who explains the politics of sidewalk cartooning: ''You can have cartoons about any of the parties, but you mustn't put anything in favor of Socialism, because the police won't stand it. Once I did a cartoon of a boa constrictor marked Capital swallowing a rabbit marked Labour. The copper came along and saw it, and he says, 'You rub that out, and look sharp about it.' ''

In book reviews, Orwell praised the radicalism of Byron, Melville, and others.

Yet Orwell shied away from outright socialism for nearly a decade. Gifted with unusual awareness of the psychologies impeding the left, Orwell needed to feel certain that the revolutionary cause was credible. This assurance he derived from contact with workers in France, England, and Spain . . .

The books written before the socialist *Road to Wigan Pier* of 1936 are highly interesting, if uneven in quality. They reveal the slow, faltering steps Orwell took *en route* to socialism, and they also show his persistent concern with work, poverty, and emotional survival.

The central theme of each early novel is the profound difficulty of breaking from established habits. Each lead character is a minor member of the lower uppercrust who tries, and fails, to find a new identity when old formulas lose their persuasive power.

Books and Themes

Flory, we saw, evolved away from the oppressive narrow-mindedness of his English enclave, only to find himself too immersed in corrupt habits to rebel effectually. In *A Clergyman's Daughter,* Dorothy Hare finds the stultifying narrowness of her Anglican routines too restraining to permit a change of life when her faith vanishes. And miserable Gordon Comstock in *Keep the Aspidistra Flying* reverts to ladder-climbing in the business world after his effort to evade ''the money-god'' proves histrionic. *Coming Up For Air* (1939) and *1984* (1949) also follow this pattern.

Orwell's early novels have obvious weaknesses. Implausible plots abound. *Down and Out in Paris and London* is less, as its title promises, a tale of two cities, than two tales of cities: Paris is the focus of one story, while London is the site of another. In *Burmese Days,* meanwhile, everything happens anti-providentially—at the worst possible moment. *A Clergyman's Daughter* is even less credible. ''Very disconnected as a whole, and rather unreal''—this was how Orwell ruefully evaluated a book which falls into five distinct sections, each with its own style and tempo.

Finally, *Keep the Aspidistra Flying* is too sour and repetitious to be readily enjoyable; portraying a bilious character in his own self-pitying accents yields unpleasant results.

Orwell later indicted himself for not being a "real novelist." He poured scorn on the early novels, in particular, dismissing them as "full of purple passages."

This is too harsh. A few of Orwell's novels are well-realized in every respect, and even the least successful (say, *A Clergyman's Daughter*) has parts far superior to the whole.   Some of Orwell's early writing *is* suspect—

for example, his frequent snack-food similes: "a lukewarm sea that foamed like coca-cola" (*Burmese Days*), "like a wind from oceans of cool beer" (*Clergyman's Daughter*), and—outdoing himself—"the dry, drifted leaves were strewn all down the pavement, crinkly and golden, like the rustling flakes of some American breakfast cereal; as though the queen of Brobdingnag had upset her packet of Truweet Breakfast Crisps down the hillside" (*Aspidistra*).

Lady Poverty

Down and Out in Paris and London is an exceptionally concise, effective fictionalization of Orwell's life at the ragged edge of poverty at the brink of "a decade of unparalleled depression." Its deft, thoughtful approach prefigures Orwell's later books on coal mining and the Spanish civil war.

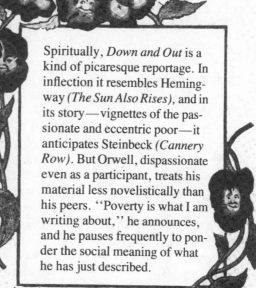

Spiritually, *Down and Out* is a kind of picaresque reportage. In inflection it resembles Hemingway *(The Sun Also Rises)*, and in its story—vignettes of the passionate and eccentric poor—it anticipates Steinbeck *(Cannery Row)*. But Orwell, dispassionate even as a participant, treats his material less novelistically than his peers. "Poverty is what I am writing about," he announces, and he pauses frequently to ponder the social meaning of what he has just described.

Focusing on the semi-proletariat leads Orwell into "the suburbs, as it were, of poverty" (where Dorothy Hare and Gordon Comstock will also be found). With benign detachment, Orwell recounts the foibles of people he clearly likes.

A CLERGYMAN'S DAUGHTER

Some thought of D. H. Lawrence's "The Daughters of the Vicar" may have contributed to this book, but its immediate inspiration seems to have been an occasion noted in *Down and Out* when "a clergyman and his daughter [were observed watching Orwell and other tramps in Lower Binfield] as though we were aquarium fishes . . ."

Now, the vicar and his daughter are inside the aquarium.

Clergyman Charles Hare is a stock figure: vague, penny-pinching, and slightly comic in his self-absorption. Hare's daughter, Dorothy, finds "chaos in her heart" when Anglicanism proves emotionally unsatisfying. Troubled by a "pagan" impulse to worship greenery and sunlight, Dorothy jabs herself with needles when she finds her mind wandering during prayer.

But mortification of the flesh proves unavailing. When Dorothy recovers from amnesia to find her body wandering, too, she realizes that her faith has evaporated. Yet she perseveres, with neither self-pity nor alarm.

"I shall go on, just as before. It's what I'm most used to." Inarticulately, Dorothy senses that ". . . though her faith had left her, the spiritual background of her mind had not changed. She did not want to change, nor could she change. Her cosmos, though it now seemed empty and meaningless, was still in a sense the Christian cosmos; the Christian way of life was still the way of life that came most naturally to her."

For a relatively uneducated 28-year-old 'spinster' of Dorothy's class and background, the only accepted alternative to renewed, faithless service to her improvident father is marriage. But Dorothy is aberrant—like Freud's Dora she is sexually repelled by men (whom she often likes, but perceives as horrible furry satyrs). A friend, Mr. Warburton, explains to Dorothy why she lost her memory (while amiably proposing):

''You'd built yourself a life-pattern—if you'll excuse a bit of psychological jargon—that was only possible for a believer. Naturally it was a strain on you since you no longer believed. Loss of memory is a device, unconsciously used, to escape from impossible situations . . .''

Warburton paints a clearly accurate picture of the straitened routines to which Dorothy's life will dwindle without marriage. (Marriage is no panacea—but it offers Dorothy prospects otherwise unattainable). She quails at the very idea: ''She could never marry. Nothing would ever overcome her horror of *all that*—at the very thought of it something within her seemed to shrink and freeze.''

Orwell's explanation is classically psychoanalytic: ''. . . though her sexual coldness seemed to her natural and inevitable, she knew well enough how it had begun. She vividly remembered certain dreadful scenes between her father and mother when she was no more than nine years old.

''These had left a deep, secret wound in her mind; then a little later, she had been frightened by some old steel engravings of nymphs pursued by satyrs . . . She recoiled. Furry thighs of satyrs!''

This is very important for interpreting Orwell's perspective. It reveals an essentially Freudian outlook; a vein of something like existentialism (*à la* James Joyce—interpreted, by Orwell, as confronting the same problem in *Ulysses* that Dorothy confronts here); and a clue both about Orwell's early resistance to socialism, and about why he was later such a free-thinking socialist.

In every novel, Orwell portrays characters who seem to be immutably tied to outworn but emotionally binding lives. Dorothy Hare loses her faith, but—paradoxically—decides to go through the motions of "serving God." Gordon Comstock briefly rejects the "money-god," but eventually falls victim to its magnetic attraction. Flory, a "most holy god" to his Burmese retainers, fails to break from the privileges and corruptions of his lordly role.

"Wrong ways of life" prove powerfully compelling. A major reason for this, says Orwell, is that many people are characterologically inflexible thanks, in part, to sexual disturbance. This is at least implicit in every novel, starting with *Burmese Days*. It is particularly clear in *A Clergyman's Daughter*.

THE EXISTENTIALIST ORWELL

Dorothy's sexual plight leaves her in a spiritual quandary. Yet, ultimately, she finds no despair in the view which, shortly later, was to prove so terrible to the existentialists—that life without "higher meaning" is a dark absurdity.

Dorothy recognizes that without "something greater" in prospect, either heaven or Utopia, life is "dreadful." Yet Dorothy's response is not dread—not fear and trembling, or nausea.

"She did not reflect, consciously, that the solution to her difficulty lay in accepting the fact that there was no solution; that faith and no faith are very much the same provided that one is doing what is customary, useful, and acceptable."

So we arrive at a bleak conclusion, a sort of joyless hedonism with duty substituted for pleasure. In the words of the shrewd Mr. Warburton, this is "the worst of both worlds"—a hard Anglican discipline without rewards; a life of humble petitioning of God, with no heaven. Submission for its own sake . . .

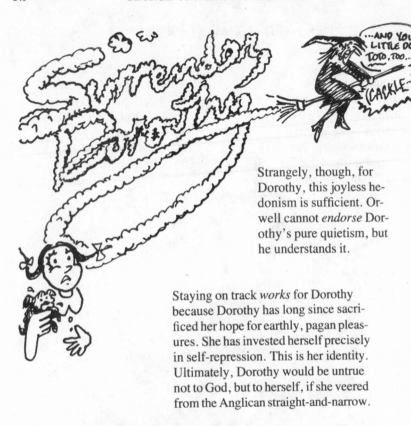

Strangely, though, for Dorothy, this joyless hedonism is sufficient. Orwell cannot *endorse* Dorothy's pure quietism, but he understands it.

Staying on track *works* for Dorothy because Dorothy has long since sacrificed her hope for earthly, pagan pleasures. She has invested herself precisely in self-repression. This is her identity. Ultimately, Dorothy would be untrue not to God, but to herself, if she veered from the Anglican straight-and-narrow.

The plenitude of her capacities for enjoyment Dorothy has converted into the religious legal tender of pleasure in self-abnegation—a kind of drab exaltation in self-denial that is the only legitimate form of fulfillment for someone, like Dorothy, committed to a "higher" realm. Even when Dorothy loses her faith, she does *not* lose her identity as one who finds repressed satisfaction in faithful service.

This solution—"no solution"—is strictly personal, an approach effective only for someone (like Dorothy) with a life already tied to devotional routine. For such a person, however, it is genuinely effective, whether a "wrong way of life" or not.

SERVING FALSE MASTERS

Here we have an early answer from Orwell to that basic
question, why do people serve false masters? Simply, says
Orwell, because they can do no other. When the ethic of
service (and servitude) becomes emotionally ingrained and
habitual, it takes more than a changed outlook to yield a
changed life. Even false masters *recognized* as such will be
served when servitude is a psychological need.

> "Beliefs change, thoughts change, but there is
> some inner part of the soul that does not change.
> Faith vanishes, but the need for faith remains
> the same as before."

A changed outlook, rather than provoking a welcome
change in habits, is likely to be *resisted*, as an incitement to dangerous new ways. Thus, Dorothy finds
herself profoundly uneasy about her liberation from
constraining faith. She had been comfortable with her
discomfort, satisfied with her narrow satisfactions.
Freedom with no clear objective leaves her without
moorings—not free for self-realization, but "free"
from the habitual tyranny she had learned to love.

My God!

Given this, the sound of the breaking
chain alarms Dorothy. With eminent
practicality, she mends it. This is her
way.

Yet even for Dorothy there is a flaw in this renewed commitment to servitude. Going through the motions without redeeming faith is a sad second-best alternative, an imperfect resolution of Dorothy's inner conflict. Faith had been the heartbeat of her existence:

">". . . given only faith, how can anything else matter? How can anything dismay you if only there is some purpose in the world which you can serve, and which, while serving it, you can understand? Your whole life is illumined by that sense of purpose. There is no weariness in your heart, no doubt, no feeling of futility, no Baudelairean *ennui* waiting for unguarded hours. Every act is significant, every moment sanctified, woven by faith as into a pattern, a fabric of never-ending joy."

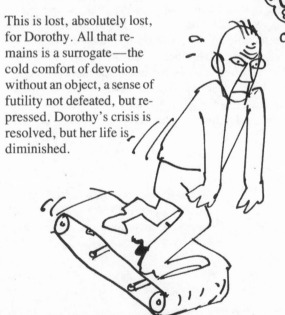

This is lost, absolutely lost, for Dorothy. All that remains is a surrogate—the cold comfort of devotion without an object, a sense of futility not defeated, but repressed. Dorothy's crisis is resolved, but her life is diminished.

What, then, about people less firmly committed to repression? Each of Orwell's later novels deals with this question, beginning with *Keep the Aspidistra Flying*.

MONEY ÜBER ALLES

Keep the Aspidistra Flying
is a complex book. Pathetic
Gordon Comstock, the anti-
hero, is simultaneously a
prism for Orwell's anti-
commercial feelings, and a
warning against blaming the
victims of commercial
civilization.

Comstock knows that, in capitalist society, money is god, and he
hopes to evade its lure. But his revolt is feeble, based more on a
jeering attitude towards "middle-class respectability" than on a profound wish to defy money and its power.

To a certain extent Orwell shares a jeering attitude towards
conventional respectability, symbolized by the potted aspidistra. The slogan "Keep the aspidistra flying" first appears in
the Trafalgar Square scene in *A Clergyman's Daughter*, when
the temporarily amnesiac Dorothy overhears a defrocked par-
son singing it mockingly to the tune "Deutschland, Deutschland über alles."

Orwell despises the pretense that submission to money-culture
is the fulfillment of Renaissance hopes. The sham humanitari-
anism of popular middle-brow literature, for example, is
skewered in scenes like the following (where bookstore clerk
Comstock butters up a regular customer):

" 'What I feel, Mr. Comstock, is that there's something so *big*
about Galsworthy. He's so broad, so universal, and yet at the
same time so thoroughly English in spirit, so *human*. His books
are real *human* documents.' 'And Priestley, too,' said Gordon.
'I think Priestley's such an awfully fine writer, don't you?'
'Oh, he is! So big, so broad, so human! And so essentially
English.' "

In an era so small, so narrow, and so inhuman, Orwell finds the banal breadth of commercial literature cloying. So does Gordon Comstock. But where Comstock sees only the cloying, rococo façade—the pretense, the aspidistra—Orwell sees also the real dignity involved in making the best of a bad situation. Kneeling before the money-god may be demeaning, but if love and family responsibility require this, there is a kind of nobility in it. Scurrying about in the rat race is, for most people, the only way to live a decent life.

Comstock dissents. Small, ''moth-eaten,'' nearly 30, and ostensibly a poet, Gordon Comstock wants to escape the ''crawling reverence for money.'' Gordon abandons a successful but unwanted career as an advertising copywriter ''to write''—to be a poet. He accepts menial clerking jobs. He refuses to marry his girlfriend, Rosemary. ''*Against* the money-god,'' Gordon writes for a magazine called *Antichrist*; though it would perhaps be more *à propos* if it were called *Antimoney*. Poverty is his badge of honor.

But Gordon, like Dorothy, does not really have an alternative in mind. ''Poetry'' is an abstraction to him, simply a negation of money-life. ''Against money'' but ''damnably selfish''—unconcerned about the involuntarily poor, jeering at socialism— Gordon is not *for* anything in particular. Without ''something greater'' in mind, Gordon remains a planet in orbit around the money-star. Negative preoccupation is still preoccupation. When Rosemary's pregnancy forces the issue, Gordon finds (to quickly abating horror) that his mock resistance is at an end. ''All his hesitation had been a kind of make-believe. He felt as though some force outside himself were pushing him.'' With a feeling of relief, Gordon returns to copywriting.

rwell concludes *Aspidistra* with an ambivalent paean of praise for the everyday decency bound up in concern for family. He is ambivalent because he does not see peace with the money-god as a positive virtue. Resignation to servitude for the sake of family may be admirable, but note well:

Gordon enters a prostituted field with a "cynical, blinkered business mentality." Advertising is simply "writing lies" to lure money from wage-earners. There is scant nobility in surrendering to *this* unholy god. *This* god actually rules, and does great harm. Money, or the lack of money, blights the lives of innumerable people.

Also, as Gordon senses, the universe ruled by the money-god is *en route* to disaster. Frequently, Gordon visualizes the aerial bombing and destruction impending in the next European war (this was in 1936). He shows prescience in this, and knows that the money-god is responsible: competition for economic power yields a harvest of death, as well as daily servitude. A decent private life may be honorable, but honor will not save us. Resistance is the implied need. A "wrong way of life" must be *changed* when it threatens war and devastation.

"Something greater" than service to the money-god is called for—and "something greater" than business civilization must be created if civilization is to survive.

Claiming that money has largely replaced God, Orwell resembles Marx. Compare the following passages:

Marx: "... the 'strange God' [of commerce] perched himself side by side with the old divinities of Europe on the altar, and one fine day threw them all overboard with a shove and a kick. It proclaimed the making of profit as the ultimate and sole purpose of mankind."

Orwell: "... money-worship has been elevated into a religion. Perhaps it is the only real religion—the only really *felt* religion—that is left to us. Money is what God used to be."

Compare, also, two poems—one by "Gordon Comstock," the other by Shakespeare (cited by Marx in an essay known to Orwell):

"Gold? yellow, glittering,
  precious gold? . . .
This yellow slave
Will knit and break religions;
  bless th'accurst;
Make the hoar leprosy ador'd;
  place thieves,
And give them title, knee, and
  approbation,
With senators on the
  bench . . ."

"We kneel before our rightful lord;/The lord of all, the money-god,/Who rules us blood and hand and brain,/ Who spies with jealous, watchful care,/Our thoughts, our dreams, our secret ways,/ Who picks our words and cuts our clothes,/And maps the pattern of our days . . ."

Shakespeare

Comstock

If anything, Orwell's poem is more comprehensive than Shakespeare's. It reveals the concern familiar from Orwell's later writings with total power, attributing this power not (here) to Big Brother, but to money. Money rules, and is worshipped "rightfully."

Money *does* have magic powers, and lack of money renders
people powerless—unless they revolt. Revolt
is made difficult, however, by the widespread tendency
to obey the money-god's commandments.

What are the principal tenets of
the new religion?

"For the employed—the slaves
and underlings—'Thou shalt not
lose they job.' "

"For employers—the money-
priesthood—'Thou shalt make
money.' "

ACCUMULATE!
ACCUMULATE!
THAT IS
MOSES AND
THE PROPHETS
TO THE
CAPITALIST!

Compare, finally, what
Marx and Orwell say
about the impact of money
on individuals:

Orwell: "He had a sort of charm, a glamour,
like all moneyed people. Money and charm;
who shall separate them? For money buys all
virtues. If you have no money, men won't
care for you, women won't love you. Money-
less, you are unlovable. Give me not
righteousness, O Lord, give me money, only
money."

Money also blesses its *owners* with lordly powers:

"Gordon had a vision of London, of the Western world; he saw a thousand million slaves toiling and grovelling about the throne of money."

"The earth is ploughed, ships sail, miners sweat in dripping tunnels under-ground, clerks hurry for the 8:15 with the fear of the boss eating at their vit-als. And even in bed with their wives they tremble and obey. Obey whom? The money-priesthood, the pink-faced masters of the world. The Upper Crust."

Here we see the apocalyp-tic voice of the later Orwell clearly prefigured.

Orwell's point here is not so much that bosses com-mand, but that workers *obey*. Would it make a difference if workers knew "that they were only puppets dancing when money pulled the strings"? Not necessar-ily: "They are too busy being born, being mar-ried, begetting, working, dying."

To change, one must not only see through false gods, but be able to stop serving them. Finding energy and hopefulness for the effort this requires is no easy matter.

Still, dangers of great enough magnitude *re-quire* changed habits. The ILP view that revolu-tion will be precipitated by war, not economic crisis, begins to creep into Orwells' outlook.

"Presently the aeroplanes are coming. In imag-ination he saw them coming now; squadron after squadron, innumerable, darkening the sky like clouds of gnats. Zoom—whizz—crash!

The whole western world going up in a roar." Unless, that is, the "reverberations of future wars" provoke a reaction *against* this "great death-wish of the modern world."

The power and malignancy of money-culture is sharply etched in Orwell's early novels. He shows few illusions about big business. In *Aspidistra*, Gran'pa Comstock is summarized as "a tough old scoundrel, who plundered the proletariat and the foreigner of fifty thousand pounds." In *A Clergyman's Daughter*, the town of Knype Hill is shown to be politically as well as economically subservient to Mr. Blifil-Gordon, proprietor of the sugar-beet refinery which employs more than half the townspeople. A marvelous scene unfolds with Blifil-Gordon in an open car, as a Conservative candidate for office, waving to the crowd, his expression "all honey and butter" . . .

Note, also, the sardonic portrayal of advertising culture in *Aspidistra*. Everywhere Gordon Comstock turns, he finds ads that "rankle in the public consciousness like a poisoned arrow." He marvels over their "vigorous badness" . . .

At first Orwell resisted the idea that "plundered proletarians" could unite to foil the money-god and avert aerial destruction. His views changed as the result of acquaintance with workers and tramps.

JOINING THE PEOPLE

When Eric Blair ventured into the seething working-class streets of London's East End in 1927 disguised as a tramp, he retraced the steps of another writer. In 1902, the already-famous Jack London—at 26 just two years older than Eric Blair in 1927—had embarked on a voyage of discovery amid the East End poor. London's great book, *The People of the Abyss*, memorably records the impressive lessons of this expedition.

Eric Blair had read *The People of the Abyss* in school and had been profoundly affected.

Still another talented writer had made a similar pilgrimage in 1842; 24-year-old Friedrich Engels, whose two years in working-class England were analyzed in *The Condition of the Working-Class in England in 1844*. An early text of Marxism, Engels' book is far wider in scope than *People of the Abyss* and far more radical than Orwell's early writings. Nevertheless, taken together, the three narratives present a remarkably cohesive picture of the English proletariat and its ragged, wandering fringe . . .

Engels: "*Working men! I have lived long enough amidst you to know something of your circumstances— your homes, your everyday life, your struggles against your oppressors. I gave up the dinner-parties and the champagne of the middle-classes. I am glad and proud to have done so.*"

London: "I went down into the under-world of London with an attitude I may best liken to that of an explorer. I went to be convinced by the evidence of my eyes, and I took certain simple criteria: that which made for life, for health, was good; that which dwarfed and distorted life was bad."

Orwell: "I felt that I had to escape from every form of man's dominion over man. I wanted to submerge myself among the oppressed, to be one of them and on their side against their tyrants."

Orwell: 'Why do tramps exist at all? Curiously, few people know that a tramp takes to the road not because he likes it, but because there happens to be a law compelling him to do so. A destitute man can only get relief at casual wards…"

London: "…called 'spikes'…"

Orwell: "And since each spike will admit him for only one night, he is automatically kept moving."

Engels: *"The New Poor Law of 1834 abolished all jobless money and provisions; the only relief allowed is admission to the workhouses ("Poor Law Bastilles," as the people call them). These are so atrocious that they frighten away anyone with hope outside. The food is worse than that of the most ill-paid working man. Tobacco is forbidden."*

London: "You tobacco users, take heed: we had to surrender our tobacco as we entered!"

Orwell: "Since we knew that the porter never searched below the knee, we hid our tobacco in our boots."

Engels: *"The workhouse is also a jail. To eat, you must finish your assigned task. To go out, you must ask permisison, which is granted or not according to the inspector's whim."*

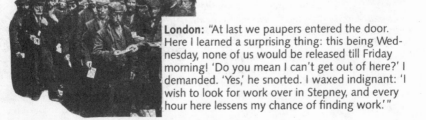

London: "At last we paupers entered the door. Here I learned a surprising thing: this being Wednesday, none of us would be released till Friday morning! 'Do you mean I can't get out of here?' I demanded. 'Yes,' he snorted. I waxed indignant: 'I wish to look for work over in Stepney, and every hour here lessens my chance of finding work.'"

Engels: *"Workhouse inmates are compelled to work at useless tasks. They break stone and pick oakum."*

Orwell: "The work was peeling potatoes for dinner—but it was a mere formality, to keep us occupied."

London: "It was sheer robbery by the authorities. The same amount of labor for a private employer would bring a better wage."

PICKING OAKUM IN THE CASUAL WARD.

Engels: *"Can anyone wonder that the poor often decline to accept public relief? That they starve rather than enter these Bastilles?"*

Orwell: "Salvation Army shelters, though clean, are far drearier than the worst lodging houses. There is such hopelessness there."

London: "Forced to wait on their feet, and faint from hunger, they yearn not for salvation, but for grub. The 'soul-snatchers' should study psychology."

Orwell: "'You 'ad your bun,' said one; 'you got to pay for it.' 'Pray for it, you mean. They can't even give you a cup of tea without you go down on your fucking knees for it.'"

Engels: *"You, with your complacent philanthropy, posing before the world as mighty benefactors of humanity when you return to the plundered victims the hundredth part of what belongs to them! Charity which treads the downtrodden still deeper in the dust, which demands that the degraded pariah shall first surrender his very claim to manhood, before your mercy deigns to press, in the shape of alms, the brand of degradation upon his brow."*

COURTYARD OF THE SALVATION ARMY BARRACKS
ON SUNDAY MORNING.

London: "Whence comes the chronic misery which persists even in periods of greatest prosperity?"

Engels: "The root cause is that the human being, the worker, is regarded in capitalist manufacture simply as equipment, for the use of which the manufacturer pays wages. The worker's condition is the pinnacle of social misery, thanks to the dominion of a class incurably debased by selfishness—I mean by this the bourgeoisie, the capitalist owners of factories and enterprises."

London: "There is a Chinese proverb, that if one man lives in laziness, another will die in hunger."

Engels: "For the bourgeoisie, there is no bliss save gain, no pain save losing gold. I once went into Manchester with such a bourgeois, and spoke to him of the frightful conditions there. The man listened quietly to the end, and said at the corner where we parted: 'And yet there is a great deal of money made here; good morning, sir.'"

Orwell: "The business man became dominant in the nineteenth century, and rules us still. On analysis his sole virtue turns out to be a talent for making money. We are bidden to admire him because, though he might be narrow-minded, sordid, grasping, and uncouth, he has 'grit'..."

Orwell: "The big hotels are quite merciless towards their employees, and they swindle their customers wholeheartedly, too. The same fundamental evil afflicts private schools—that they have ultimately no purpose except to make money."

Engels: *"The criminal irresponsibility of the manufacturer springs from his mania for profit. He can increase his capital only by producing commodities, for which he needs workers. Capital grows by claiming a percentage of Labor's produce. (I use Labor, working-class, and proletariat as equivalents.) Capital leaves Labor as little as Labor will allow, and uses ruthless means to keep Labor powerless. The consequence, for countless thousands, is destitution."*

London: "If civilization has increased the producing power of the average man, why has it not bettered his lot? There can be one answer only—MISMANAGEMENT.

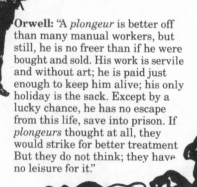

Orwell: "A *plongeur* is better off than many manual workers, but still, he is no freer than if he were bought and sold. His work is servile and without art; he is paid just enough to keep him alive; his only holiday is the sack. Except by a lucky chance, he has no escape from this life, save into prison. If *plongeurs* thought at all, they would strike for better treatment But they do not think; they have no leisure for it."

Engels:

"*The worker is helpless. If all workers decided to starve rather than be exploited, the capitalist would surrender. But alone, the worker cannot survive a single week. The bourgeoisie holds a state-protected monopoly on work, tools, land, and commodities. If the wage-slave seems free it is because he is not sold all at once, but piecemeal—by the day, the week, the year. No capitalist sells him; rather, he is forced to sell himself, to be the slave of the whole property-holding class.*"

IN CHRISTIAN ENGLAND
(*Illustrated Bits* 1885)

London: "The unfit and the unneeded! Industry does not clamor for them."

Orwell: "The number of un-employed men who are ready to do the work makes the margin-ally employed powerless to fight for better treatment."

Engels: "*If one alone refuses to work for low wages, there are dozens out of work who are thankful for the most trifling offer. When I came to Manchester in November, 1842, there were crowds of unemployed working-men at every street corner.*"

London: "The men themselves ascribe their misery to foreign immigration, especially of Polish and Russian Jews, who take their places at lower wages."

Engels: *"They do not recognize the true cause of their wretchedness, so they attribute it to all sorts of small causes. The uneducated Irish see the English as their worst enemies."*

Orwell: "Paddy had a worm-like envy of anyone better off—not of the rich, for they were beyond his social horizon, but of men in work. He pined for work as an artist pines to be famous. If he saw an old man working he would say bitterly, 'Look at dat old bastard keepin' able-bodied men out o' work'; or if it was a boy, 'It's dem young devils what's takin' de bread out of our mouths.' And all foreigners were 'dem bloody dagoes'—for, according to his theory, foreigners were responsible for unemployment."

Engels: *"It must be a source of rejoicing for the patriotic German stocking weaver that his starvation wages force his English brother to starve too!"*

London: "I stopped to listen to an argument on the Mile End Waste among workmen of the better class. They had surrounded a pleasant-faced man of thirty and were arguing rather heatedly. 'But 'ow about this 'ere cheap immigration?' one of them demanded. 'The Jews of Whitechapel, say, a-cuttin' our throats right along?' 'You can't blame them,' was the answer. 'They're just like us, and they've got to live. Don't blame the man who offers to work cheaper than you and gets your job. Wages always come down when two men are after the same job. That's the fault of competition, not of the man who cuts the price.' 'But wages don't come down when there's a union,' the objection was made. 'And there you are, right on the head.'"

Engels: *"What falls hardest upon the English working-man is the insecurity of his position. The slave is assured a bare livelihood, the serf has at least a scrap of land; but the worker must rely upon himself alone, while everything he can do is but a drop in the ocean compared with the floods of chance to which he is exposed."*

London: "Work as they will, wage-earners cannot make their future secure. It is all a matter of chance. Everything depends upon *the thing happening,* the thing about which they can do nothing. Precaution cannot fend it off, nor can wiles evade it."

Orwell: "A particularly appalling accident happened in one mine. A man who had known perfectly well that it was unsafe went to the mine anyway, in the daily expectation of an accident, but needful of work. Said a mate: 'And it worked on his mind to that extent that he got to kissing his wife before he went to work. And she told me afterwards that it were over twenty year since he'd kissed her.'"

London: "Talk of war! The mortality in the South African and Philippine wars fades to insignificance. Here, in the heart of peace, is where the blood is shed; and here women, children, and babes in arms are killed just as ferociously as men. War! In England every year 500,000 men, women, and children in the various industries are killed and disabled."

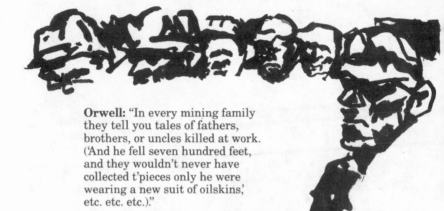

Orwell: "In every mining family they tell you tales of fathers, brothers, or uncles killed at work. ('And he fell seven hundred feet, and they wouldn't never have collected t'pieces only he were wearing a new suit of oilskins,' etc. etc. etc.)."

"Every year about one miner in nine hundred is killed and one in about six is injured; many injuries result in total disablement."

UNDERCUTTING A THIN COAL
(Margery May in the *English Illustrated Magazine* 1889)

WOMEN MINERS ON THE PIT BROW
(*Graphic* 1878)

London: "The thing happens, the father is struck down, and what then? A mother with children can do little or nothing. There is no guarding against it. It is fortuitous. A family stands so many chances of falling to the bottom of the Abyss."

Orwell: "The middle-classes still talk about 'lazy idle loafers on the dole,' and say that 'these men could all find work if they want to.' You've heard them: 'My dear, I don't *believe* all this nonsense about unemployment. Why, only last week we wanted a man to weed the garden, and we simply couldn't get one. They don't *want* to work, that's all it is.'"

Orwell: "The tragic thing is that these opinions percolate to the workers themselves. When I first saw unemployed men at close quarters, what horrified me was that many were *ashamed* of unemployment. I was very ignorant, but not so ignorant as to imagine that when the loss of foreign markets pushes two million men out of work, those two million are any more at fault than people ruined in an earthquake."

Engels: "*The 'surplus population' of England keeps body and soul together by begging, stealing, street-sweeping, collecting manure, pushing hand-carts, driving donkeys, peddling, or performing occasional small jobs. In every great town a multitude of such people may be found.*"

London: "From the slimy sidewalk, the men pick up bits of orange peel, apple skin, and grape stems —and eat them."

Engels: "*Potato parings, vegetable refuse, and rotten vegetables—everything is greedily gathered up which may possibly contain an atom of nourishment.*"

Orwell: "The scene stays in my mind: dumpy, shawled women, kneeling in the cindery mud and the bitter wind, searching eagerly for tiny chips of coal. In winter fuel is almost more important than food."

WIGAN PIER

We are now in coal-mining country.

Comissioned by the Left Book Club to report on the coal miners, Orwell boarded with miners for several months in a series of coal-country towns. He was powerfully impressed by the courage, decency, and political conviction of the miners he met, many of whom were ILP or Communist Party members. Descending into the mines, Orwell was appalled at their hazards and hardships.

Coal, Orwell reflected, fuels all creative endeavor aboveground; how ironic that the coal miners should be so nearly invisible underground . . .

To publicize the miners, Orwell researched them carefully. One miner said that Orwell resembled nothing so much as a latter-day Sherlock Holmes . . .

The Road to Wigan Pier appeared in 1937 and attracted widespread attention, both for its effective reporting and for Orwell's bull-in-a-china-shop denunciation of virtually everyone on the left—party bureaucrats, intellectuals, middle-class socialists, workers who 're-semble' middle-class socialists, vegetarians, etc.

Though many of his polemical points are patently unfair, there is nevertheless a rational kernel to Orwell's argument. This is that socialists routinely *misunderstand* workers, and thus fail to persuade them. "The trouble with all orthodox Marxists is that, possessing a system which appears to explain everything, they never bother to discover what is going on inside other people's heads."

Without real empathy for workers, socialist doctrinaires develop stereotyped and impractical ways of dealing with people.

In Catalonia the following year, Orwell gained real insight into better styles of socialist communication.

The Spanish War

When, on 18 July 1936, the Fascist generals Franco and Mola revolted against the new "Popular Front" government of Spain (a coalition of workers' and liberal capitalist parties), Orwell was heartened to see the Spanish working-class arm itself to fight back. In a few weeks it became clear that the immediate Fascist threat had been repelled and that fighting would continue indefinitely. Workers and radicalized peasants put up stiff resistance both to Franco and (more generally) to all Spanish class exploitation. Something very much like a revolution broke out, as the exploited led the war against Fascist Franco.

To Orwell, this was a beacon of hope. Fascism had been in the ascendant for some time: Mussolini had taken power in Italy in 1922, and had invaded Abyssinia (Ethiopia) in 1935; worse, Hitler had taken the helm in Germany in 1933. Germany and Italy were clearly rearming for a second World War. In general, Fascism seemed to be advancing. The Spanish resistance offered hope that, on the Iberian peninsula at least, Fascism could be halted.

Orwell decided to go to Spain. Here, too, he knew few political specifics. Events forced him to learn.

A complex fight had broken out among the anti-Franco parties in Spain—the Anarchist workers of the *Confederación Nacional de Trabajadores* (CNT); the Communists (the PSUC or *Partido Socialista Unificado de Catalunya* —a four-party 'coalition' dominated by the Communist Party and affiliated with the Communist International); and the dissident communists of the POUM, the *Partido Obrero de Unificación Marxista*. Very different paths to victory were urged: The Anarchist CNT and the POUM advocated revolutionary war—*against both* Fascism and liberal capitalism—while the Communists pushed for a worker/capitalist alliance to protect the Popular Front *status quo*—"war now, revolution later."

Orwell knew nothing of this dispute. Wanting an introduction from a left-wing party to enter Spain, he sought out Harry Pollitt, general-secretary of the British Communist Party. Pollitt, however, judged Orwell to be 'politically unreliable,' so Orwell approached Fenner Brockway of the ILP (the POUM's sister party). He thus wound up with a letter of introduction to the ILP representative in Barcelona, John McNair.

En route to Barcelona, in Paris, Orwell spent a day with writer Henry Miller— who argued that it was absurd to fight for any cause, yet gave Orwell his blessing (and a warm corduroy coat) when it became clear that Orwell could not be deterred.

Purely by the accident of this ILP recommendation, Orwell joined a POUM militia.

John McNair later recalled Orwell's arrival: a POUM sentry at McNair's door announced, "There's a great big Englishman to see you." Friendly immediately—McNair had liked *Burmese Days*—McNair and Orwell discussed Orwell's plans. McNair recommended political journalism. Orwell, though, was determined to fight. Vaguely planning to join the Communist-dominated International Brigade, Orwell was directed, instead, to the Lenin Barracks of the POUM. (He later said he might have joined the anarchist militia if he had understood the situation better.)

¡SEÑOR EL INGLÉS!

Commissioned a corporal in charge of twelve militia-men, Orwell had to hurdle a major obstacle before leaving for the front: In all of Spain, evidently, there were no size twelve military boots. Orwell ended up sending off to England for a pair . . .

Barcelona's atmosphere of worker power exhilarated Orwell, but he felt indifferent to the specific virtues of the POUM.

IF YOU HAD ASKED ME WHY I HAD JOINED THE MILITIA I SHOULD HAVE ANSWERED "TO FIGHT AGAINST FASCISM," AND IF YOU HAD ASKED ME WHAT I WAS FIGHTING FOR, I SHOULD HAVE ANSWERED "COMMON DECENCY." THE KALEIDOSCOPE OF POLITICAL PARTIES AND TRADE UNIONS, WITH THEIR TIRESOME NAMES, MERELY EXASPERATED ME. I THOUGHT IT IDIOTIC THAT PEOPLE FIGHTING FOR THEIR LIVES SHOULD HAVE SEPARATE PARTIES. MY ATTITUDE ALWAYS WAS, "WHY CAN'T WE DROP ALL THIS POLITICAL NON-SENSE AND GET ON WITH THE WAR?"

BUT IN SPAIN, ESPECIALLY IN CATALONIA, THIS PROVED TO BE AN ATTITUDE THAT NO ONE COULD OR DID KEEP UP INDEFINITELY. EVERY-ONE, HOWEVER UNWILLINGLY, TOOK SIDES SOONER OR LATER. FOR EVEN IF ONE CARED NOTHING FOR THE POLITICAL PARTIES AND THEIR "LINES," IT WAS TOO OBVIOUS THAT ONE'S OWN DESTINY WAS INVOLVED.

Soon, Orwell realized that everything that happened to him in Spain happened as it did because he belonged to the POUM. He realized that he was "a pawn in an enormous struggle between two political theories"—and that these theories *mattered*.

War without revolution, or war *and* revolution? This was the question which events posed for anti-Franco Spain. To understand this question, it is vital to picture what was happening geopolitically.

Franco's 'pro-slavery revolt'—accurately predicted by POUM leader Joaquín Maurin in Spain's parliament six weeks before it happened—differed from the Fascism of Hitler and Mussolini in one crucial respect: it was a "military mutiny backed up by the aristocracy and the Church," not a mass movement of shopkeepers and small farmers; Franco's goal was to protect feudal as well as capitalist property. Some sectors of the capitalist class so mistrusted his feudal bias that they opposed Franco—"the very people," said Orwell, "who are the supporters of Fascism when it appears in a more modern form."

The pillar of anti-Franco politics, however, was not the capitalist wing of the Popular Front, but the working-class—especially trade-union members.

The Popular Front government proved vacillating and uncertain at the time of the Fascist uprising. "The one step that could save the immediate situation, the arming of the workers, was only taken unwillingly and in response to violent popular clamor." Once armed, the workers moved swiftly to stop the Fascist advance, showing great resolve.

"It was the kind of effort that could probably only be made by people who were fighting with a revolutionary intention—*i.e.*, for something better than the *status quo*."

"Men and women armed only with sticks of dynamite rushed across the open squares and stormed stone buildings held by trained soldiers with machine-guns. Machine-gun nests that the Fascists had placed at strategic spots were smashed by rushing taxis at them at sixty miles an hour."

The goal of this initial fighting was to guarantee power for the exploited. "Spanish working-class resistance was accompanied by—one might almost say it consisted of—a definite revolutionary outbreak." Many big estates and industries were expropriated. In many places local councils of workers and peasants were formed to replace capitalists, landlords, and the old pro-business police. Many churches were destroyed.

"In Catalonia, for the first few months, most of the actual power was in the hands of the Anarcho-Syndicalists, who controlled most of the key industries. The thing that had happened in Spain was, in fact, not merely a civil war, but the beginning of a revolution."

Still, the workers did not overthrow the Popular Front government; pressure from Franco made this difficult. The immediate need seemed to be unity against Fascism.

"In essence it was a class war. If it had been won, the cause of the common people everywhere would have been strengthened."

''The war was actually won for Franco by the Germans and Italians,'' who supplied weapons, aid, and troops.

Russia was the only major power to furnish weapons to the anti-Franco forces, and did so in such a way—with strings attached—that the Spanish war was carried out in line with Russian foreign policy.

The curious fact which Orwell publicized in *Homage to Catalonia* was that, in Spain, the influence of Russian and Spanish Communism was exerted to *stop* the unfolding social revolution, not to extend it.

The reason for Russia's success in repressing the Spanish revolution is not hard to fathom. Consider the situation.

In 1933, Stalin's so-called ''Third Period'' policy of fighting all non-Communist parties bore poisonous fruit in Germany. An alliance between the powerful Socialist and Communist parties would have halted Hitler's rise to power; Stalin, saying that Socialists are ''social fascists,'' prevented this bloc. Hitler thus reached power through the divided 'red sea' of the workers' movement, both sides of which he then obliterated.

In this way the strongest party of the Communist International outside Russia was destroyed.

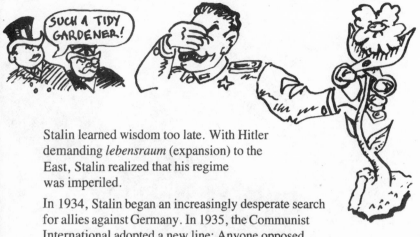

Stalin learned wisdom too late. With Hitler
demanding *lebensraum* (expansion) to the
East, Stalin realized that his regime
was imperiled.

In 1934, Stalin began an increasingly desperate search
for allies against Germany. In 1935, the Communist
International adopted a new line: Anyone opposed
to Nazism was a potential ally, even conservative
capitalists. Not revolution, but "Popular Front"
governments uniting capitalists and workers against
Fascism—this became the new strategic objective.
Internationally, Stalin sought an alliance with
England and France.

In this context the Spanish war presented Russia with a major
headache. If Franco were to win, Germany and Italy would be
further emboldened, while France would be ringed by a semi-
circle of Fascist powers. This was clearly unacceptable. No more
acceptable, however, was revolutionary war leading to socialism—since this would unalterably convince France and England
that Russia remained subversive. The only satisfactory alternative would be to defeat Fascism and revolution *at the same time*.
This would show France and England (a) that Fascism is not
invincible, and (b) that Russia is a reliably moderate ally.

All this produced a Russian policy opposed to the
Spanish Anarchists and the POUM. Appeasement of
French and British capital required victory for the pro-
capitalist wing of the Spanish Popular Front. Hence,
Orwell's conclusion:

"Official Communism must be regarded, at any
rate for the time being, as an anti-revolutionary
force."

The Anarchists were hugely popular, but even the smaller parties—*e.g.*, the POUM, "the most extreme of the revolutionary parties"—were of appreciable size: When Orwell arrived in Barcelona in January 1937, there were 70,000 POUM members active.

For workers' power: Anarchists, the POUM, most workers.

For the Popular Front: Communists, liberals, the middle-class.

The Communist-led PSUC, meanwhile, originally a tiny group, had grown to great strength with an "enormous influx largely from the middle-class—shopkeepers, officials, army officers, well-to-do peasants, etc., etc.

"By proclaiming a non-revolutionary policy the Communists were able to gather in all those whom the extremists had scared."

Orwell saw none of this at first. Barcelona was still "workers' Barcelona," with the CNT still "in virtual control." POUM leader Julián Gorkin had acclaimed Barcelona as "the new Moscow."

Orwell was impressed:

"Practically every building of any size had been seized by the workers and was draped with red flags or with the red and black

flag of the Anarchists; every wall was scrawled with the hammer and sickle and with the initials of the revolutionary parties. Waiters treated you as an equal. Servile speech had disappeared.

"Large blocks of people believed that all men are equal and acted on their belief. The result was a feeling of liberation and hope that it is difficult to conceive in our money-tainted atmosphere."

"All this was queer and moving. There was much I did not understand, in some ways I did not even like it, but I recognized it immediately as a state of affairs worth fighting for."

Joining the POUM MILITIA

In training at the Lenin Barracks in Barcelona, Orwell was amazed at "the badness of our weapons" and at the general lack of equipment. Military expertise was in equally short supply—so scarce, in fact, that Orwell wound up giving instruction.

When John McNair visited the Lenin Barracks three days after Orwell enlisted, "there was George, forcing about fifty young, enthusiastic but undisciplined Catalonians to learn the rudiments of military drill."

All told, Orwell spent 115 days at the Aragón front in the vicinity of Fascist-controlled Huesca "during the most inactive period of the war." At the end of this time Orwell received a bullet in the neck.

The POUM militia was based next to a friendly PSUC militia. "During all the time I was at the front I never once remember any PSUC adherent showing me hostility because I was POUM. That kind of thing belonged in Barcelona or in places even remoter from the war."

Orwell cut quite a figure at the front. When he was transferred to a nearby ILP militia, commander Bob Edwards reported that "All six-foot-three of him strode towards me, and his clothing was grotesque, to say the least."

"He wore corduroy riding breeches, khaki puttees, and huge muddy boots, I've never *seen* boots so large. On his shoulder he carried a rifle, on his belt two hand grenades, and running behind Orwell was a shaggy mongrel dog with 'POUM' painted on his side."

When Edwards returned to England, Orwell replaced him as ILP coordinator. Orwell is remembered by his comrades as "a much simpler person than he's made out to be, so ordinary and decent"—agreeable, light-hearted, talkative.

Aragón commandante Georges Kopp, a Belgian, said at the time that Orwell was so tall "that one needed to climb up to talk to him." (Kopp and Orwell became life-long friends.)

His POUM comrades recall Orwell as "warm and human," but so "long-legged that he always had to bend down in the trenches."

The POUM/ILP bases were several hundred yards from a Fascist encampment, with a no-man's land in the middle filled with a maze of barbed wire, trenches, and machine-gun nests. Each side held a nearly impregnable position, so that assaults were rare. On the whole, the fighting along this front had reached a point of virtual stalemate.

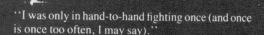

"I was only in hand-to-hand fighting once (and once is once too often, I may say)."

The Anarchists were about to spring an attack near Huesca, and the POUM militia decided to help by diverting Fascist troops away from Huesca. Two commanders, Benjamin (a 25-year-old Polish Jew) and Jorge Roca led 15 volunteers on a midnight raid. Cutting through barbed wire, wading through an irrigation ditch, and creeping "like huge black mushrooms gliding slowly forward," Benjamin, Jorge, Orwell and the others advanced.

"Benjamin, close beside me, kept whispering fiercely in my ear: 'To keep ze head down! To keep ze head down!' "

Hurling grenades over the Fascist parapet, the raiders were greeted by a volley of rifle fire which "momentarily put everything in lurid light."

"Benjamin kneeled with a pleased, devilish expression on his face and fired back. By a stroke of luck I dropped a bomb almost exactly where the machine-gun flashed. Instantly there was a diabolical outcry of screams and groans. Poor wretch! Poor wretch! I felt a vague sorrow."

After capturing the Fascist base, the POUM invaders were routed by several hundred Fascist reinforcements—who were, in this way, diverted from Huesca.

"I learned now that you can *always* run when you think you have fifty or a hundred armed men after you—no matter how wet, cold, or tired."

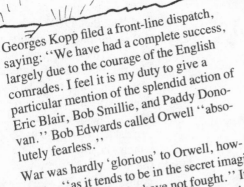

Georges Kopp filed a front-line dispatch, saying: "We have had a complete success, largely due to the courage of the English comrades. I feel it is my duty to give a particular mention of the splendid action of Eric Blair, Bob Smillie, and Paddy Donovan." Bob Edwards called Orwell "absolutely fearless."

War was hardly 'glorious' to Orwell, however—"as it tends to be in the secret imaginations of people who have not fought." It was, rather, principally a matter of "mud, lice, hunger, and cold."

When Eileen, now assisting McNair in Barcelona, managed to send chocolates and tea to the front, it was a memorable occasion.

Dearest,
You are a wonderful wife.
When I saw the cigars
my heart melted away.

Sometimes, the Aragón spring was beautiful. Orwell remarks on the "wild roses with pink blooms the size of saucers that straggled over the shell-holes," and recalls once, at the mules' drinking pool, finding "exquisite green frogs the size of a penny, so brilliant that the young grass looked dull beside them." Generally, though, the reality was boredom, dirt, and hills "like grey wrinkled elephant skin."

To fill the becalmed hours at the front, the POUM and ILP *camaradas* talked politics. For Orwell, this was a trial since "the political side of the war bored me. The inter-party feud was annoying and I tended to react against the viewpoint of which I heard most—*i.e.,* the POUM–ILP viewpoint."

Says Bob Edwards: "I found it very difficult to convince Orwell that the civil war in Spain was essentially a political conflict—a conflict of ideas.

More impressive to Orwell than formal argumentation was the social equality and voluntary discipline of the revolutionary militia. "I was isolated among the most revolutionary section of the Spanish working-class. There were officers, but there was no military rank in the ordinary sense; no titles, no badges, no saluting. The militias were a sort of temporary working model of the classless society; there wasn't perfect equality, but there was a nearer approach to it than I would have thought conceivable.

Circumstances did not permit Orwell to stand above the inter-party feud very long. His return to Barcelona just before May Day, 1937, presented him with an inescapable choice.

The fighting since June 1936 had carried matters to an unstable equilibrium. Much private property had been expropriated, yet governmental power remained in the hands of the Popular Front. Were the gains of the workers to be extended? Or would the pro-capitalist parties prevent this? Orwell wavered, siding first with the Popular Front . . .

Said the Communists: "At present, nothing matters except winning the war. We can't afford to alienate the well-to-do by talk of revolution. Above all, to be efficient, we must do away with revolutionary chaos. We need a strong government and a fully militarized army. Clinging to workers' control is worse than useless; it is counter-revolutionary, since it leads to divisions which help the Fascists. At this stage, we are fighting not for the dictatorship of the proletariat, but for parliamentary democracy."

The counterargument was also strong:

Said the POUM: "It is nonsense to talk of opposing Fascism by bourgeois 'democracy,' since both are forms of capitalism; 'democracy' all too often turns *into* Fascism (as in Italy and Germany). The only real alternative to Fascism is workers' control. If you pursue any lesser goal, you will either demoralize the workers and peasants upon whom victory depends, or you will 'succeed' only in restoring capitalist business-as-usual. If the workers do not control the armed forces, the armed forces will control the workers. The war and the revolution are inseparable!"

Adjudicating between these views is supremely difficult, since each offers not only a different principle, but a different assessment of specific facts. If it were possible to say conclusively that revolutionary war would fail to defeat Franco, the Communist position would gain credibility. If, on the other hand, it could be incontrovertibly shown that revolutionary war would yield victory, while non-revolutionary war would not, then the POUM/Anarchist view would be vindicated. But the intricate realities of the geopolitical situation rendered both views factually uncertain.

Events, however, gave the lie to PSUC rhetoric. "On paper the Communist case was a good one, but their actual behavior made it difficult to believe in their good faith. The oft-repeated slogan: 'The war first, the revolution afterwards,' was eye-wash (though devoutly believed in by the average PSUC militia-man). The PSUC worked not to postpone the Spanish revolution, but to make sure it never happened. This became obvious as power was twisted out of working-class hands and as revolutionaries of every shade were flung into jail."

Fundamentally, in Victor Serge's succinct phrase, "it was not a matter of persuasion: it was a matter of murder."

Victor Serge, 1890–1947

The process which led to the jailing of revolutionaries and the restoration of private property started innocuously. Step by step, the government persuaded the workers to surrender first one gain, then another. ''The workers could always be persuaded by saying, 'Unless you go along, we shall lose the war.' ''

Still, until May 1937, the CNT and its worker following retained the bulk of power in Barcelona. A showdown was required to expropriate this power.

When Orwell arrived in Barcelona on the eve of May Day, he had no inkling of what was about to transpire. When May Day passed in a ''strange silence''—party tensions prevented a celebration—Orwell felt ''as though some huge evil intelligence were brooding over the town.''

But his primary goal was rest and relaxation. Eileen wrote to her brother Laurence on May Day that ''George is here on leave. He arrived completely ragged, almost barefoot, a little lousy, dark brown and looking very well. In the previous twelve hours he had been in trains consuming muscatel, brandies, and chocolate.''

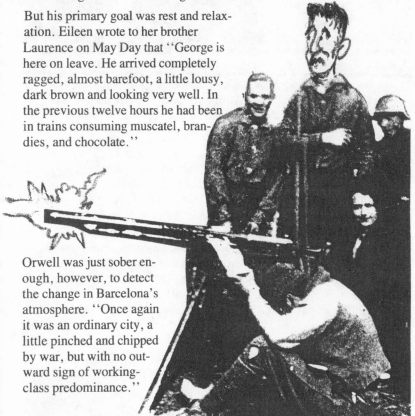

Orwell was just sober enough, however, to detect the change in Barcelona's atmosphere. ''Once again it was an ordinary city, a little pinched and chipped by war, but with no outward sign of working-class predominance.''

GEORGE AND EILEEN WITH ILP MILITIA MEMBERS

What did this betoken? The answer was clear in less than a week.

Antonov-Ovseyenko (right) and Russian Naval Officers on the way to Spain.

It was purely by accident that Orwell witnessed what ensued. His scheduled early return to the front was delayed by a characteristic problem. "I had to wait while the bootmakers made me a new pair of boots big enough to fit me."

What did Orwell's big feet stumble into? A tangled situation in which the Spanish Communists took orders from two emissaries of Stalin: Antonov-Ovseyenko, leader of the 1917 assault on the Tsar's Winter Palace (later to perish as a "Trotskyist" in Stalin's purges); and Hungarian Ernö Serö. According to Jesús Hernández, Communist minister in the Spanish government, Antonov-Ovseyenko and Serö decided to provoke a fight in an effort to discredit the CNT and the POUM. Victor Serge, the great revolutionary writer, heard advance warnings of this: " In April, I scattered my futile warnings in the left-wing Socialist press."
The Russians had leverage in Spain thanks to the weapons they supplied. People in positions of influence (*e.g.*, in the government) were very reluctant to endanger the flow of arms.

The Persecution of Radicals

The special importance of Russian arms was immediately apparent to Orwell on the Barcelona streets. After months on the front with scarcely any weapons at all, Orwell was surprised to see government Assault Guards—a kind of special police force—handsomely equipped (even with sub-machine guns).

Meanwhile, the government had ordered all citizens to hand in their weapons; trade-unionists in particular were to be disarmed. "Naturally, this order was not obeyed; the Anarchists' weapons could only be taken from them by force."

On 3 May 1937, without warning, Assault Guards tried to seize the Barcelona Telephone Exchange from the workers who controlled it. The workers resisted, and were joined in the streets by many others.

"It is probable that the emotion that brought people into the streets resembled the emotion that had led them to resist the rebel generals. The issue seemed clear enough: On one side, the CNT, on the other, the police."

"I have no particular love for the idealized 'worker,' but when I see an actual flesh-and-blood worker in conflict with his natural enemy, the policeman, I do not have to ask which side I am on."

SIGNALEMENT

Taille	**1.82**
Front	**moy.**
Nez	**rect.**
Bouche	**moy;**
Menton	**rond**
Visage	**ovale**
Cheveux	**cht.**
Barbe	**rasée**
Corpulence	**moy.**
Yeux	**cht.**
Teint	**clair**

The fighting in Barcelona took an odd turn. In a flash,
the city was partitioned into sectors controlled by the
various parties. Much like the front, every sector flew
a party flag. The Ramblas, the working-class district,
was in Anarchist hands.

Sporadic fighting took place for four days,
with barricades erected in strategic spots.
When Orwell reported to POUM Headquarters he was assigned guard duty. There
was occasional sniper fire, but little open
fighting. A total of 400 people were killed in
Barcelona during this period, but not many
died in one place or at one time. No one
wanted a full-scale civil war inside the civil
war.

From his post atop the Poliorama cinema—adjacent to
PSUC Headquarters at the Hotel Colon, where a machine-
gun loomed from an upstairs window—Orwell watched in
"concentrated anger, disgust, and fury" as the inconclusive
contest unfolded. The workers wanted to recover the Telephone Exchange, but the Assault Guards were too well
armed to be overcome. Meanwhile, the POUM role was
strictly defensive: no militia-men were called back from the
front, and Orwell was instructed to fire only in reply to direct
attacks. "The POUM leaders took the rather pedantic
Marxist line that when the workers are in the streets it is the
duty of the revolutionary leaders to be with them." But the
workers had few clear objectives. Stalemate again.

The logjam was ultimately broken by outside intervention. From the Poliorama rooftop, Orwell had an excellent view of the ''glittering, pale blue sea'' of the Barcelona harbor— where on 5 May British warships hovered into sight; a rumor circulated that foreign intervention was imminent.

''It did seem inherently likely that the British government, which had not raised a finger to save the Spanish Republic from Franco, would intervene quickly enough to save it from its own working class.''

Whether Orwell would have fought the British Navy had this occurred is a question that cannot be answered—since two days later 6000 Assault Guards from Valencia sailed into the harbor to subdue the city.

The CNT submitted—a step marking a basic change in CNT orientation. In the words of the eminent Anarchist historian, José Peirats, ''there was a re-nunciation of the revolution.'' Submission to the Popular Front government seemed to be the better part of valor.

The POUM, still committed to revolutionary war, was to be the next target of PSUC-inspired repression.

Two days after the shooting stopped, Orwell wrote to an English friend: "I greatly hope to come out of this alive, if only to write a book about it." He did survive—but by the skin of his teeth.

General Franco.
der Führer der spanisch nationalen Militärgruppe.

Orwell had applied to join the Communist-controlled International Brigade in Madrid. Now, however, deciding that this was out of the question—"sooner or later it might mean being used against the Spanish working-class—Orwell returned to the POUM front. Although convinced that the Communists would impose some kind of dictatorship over the workers, Orwell decided that "it did not follow that the Government was not worth fighting for. The only alternative was an infinitely worse dictatorship by Franco, who was tied to the big feudal landlords and stood for clerico-military reaction." Franco was also tied to German and Italian Fascism.

Orwell's war was cut short when, at dawn on 20 May, he was felled by a bullet from a German Mauser. After spending time in a POUM Sanatorium, Orwell returned to Barcelona. A vocal cord was paralyzed, which made it hard to speak: "I also can't sing, but people tell me this doesn't matter." Otherwise, Orwell was fine.

Around the start of Franco's rebellion in 1936, Trotsky had sent Victor Serge a clipping from *Pravda,* the main Soviet newspaper, announcing the beginning of the Russian purge trials: "The monsters, enemies of the people, will be annihilated with a mighty hand." Trotsky wrote: "I fear this may be the prelude to a massacre." The massacre which followed extended to Spain.

> *Pravda* declared in December 1936 that "In Catalonia the elimination of Trotskyites and Anarcho-Syndicalists has begun. It will be carried out with the same energy as in the Soviet Union." This friendly announcement proved slightly pre-mature, but, by the time Orwell returned to Barcelona in June, the "elimination" campaign was well under way.

"When I got to the hotel lounge Eileen rose in a very unconcerned manner and, with a sweet smile, hissed in my ear: *'Get out!'* 'What?' 'Get out of here *at once!'* 'What?' 'Listen! You must get outside quickly before they ring up the police.' "

" 'What the devil is this all about?' I asked when we reached the pavement. 'Haven't you *heard?* The POUM's been suppressed. Practically every-one's in prison. And they say they're shooting people al-ready.' "

POUM members and other revolutionaries were accused of "Trotskyism." This, in the nether logic of the Communist International, amounted to a charge of Fascism. Spanish Communist Party secretary José Diaz announced the new line on 9 May: "Our principle enemies are the Fascists. However, these include not only the Fascists themselves, but also the Trotskyites . . . . If the government knows this, why doesn't it treat them like Fascists and exterminate them pitilessly?" This is precisely what Stalin had undertaken in Russia . . .

Vile propaganda poured forth to justify the persecution of all who continued to argue that "the war and the revolution are inseparable." Orwell reported that Barcelona was covered with PSUC posters showing the POUM as a leftist "un-masked" to reveal a hideous figure marked with a swastika.

"Scores of thousands of working-class people, including eight or ten thousand soldiers freezing in front-line trenches, were declared to be simply traitors in the pay of the enemy."

In retaliation, Orwell chalked the slogan "¡Viva POUM!" on every available wall.

¡Viva POUM!

POUM leader Andrés Nin was arrested on 15 June and murdered in prison. Nin had been Secretary of the Red International of Labor Unions, a political prisoner in pre-revolutionary Spain, Justice Minister in the revolutionary Catalan government, and a critical admirer of Trotsky.

"Nearly all our friends and acquaintances are in jail . . ." Among thousands arrested were José Rovira, POUM general at the front; Georges Kopp, who later escaped; Bob Smillie, who died in prison, and many others.

"Smillie's death is not a thing I can easily forgive."

Orwell found the POUM purist and somewhat boring, but there was "less than no evidence" of Fascism. "I myself never joined the POUM—for which afterwards, when they were suppressed, I was rather sorry."

Eileen and George went into hiding. A few weeks later they crossed the frontier with John McNair and Stafford Cottman. ILP leader Fenner Brockway met them at the French border.

Thus did the Stalinist bureaucracy free itself to manipulate the Spanish working-class. Franz Borkenau, Orwell's friend, concluded that "this fight between revolutionary Anarchists and non-revolutionary Communists was inevitable, because fire and water cannot mix." For the time being, water prevailed.

"Curiously enough, the whole experience has left me with not less but more belief in the decency of human beings." This was Orwell's summation in *Homage to Catalonia*, published in 1938.

Homage is a wonderfully balanced document, both political and personal. In 1938, however, few people saw this. Less than 2000 copies sold. Still, Emma Goldman wrote to Rudolf Rocker that, at last, "someone outside our ranks has painted the Spanish anarchists as they really are"; Trotskyist Reg Groves called *Homage* "the best thing that ever happened to us"; and perceptive readers such as Franz Borkenau and Herbert Read extended congratulations.

In Spain, the revolution had been betrayed and the war lost—two events which Orwell felt were linked. Nevertheless, Orwell felt that future wars and revolutions could be won. Neither Fascism nor Stalinism is invincible: "If the problems of western capitalism are to be solved, it will be through a third alternative—a genuinely revolutionary movement, willing to make drastic changes (using violence if necessary) without losing touch with democracy. Such a thing is by no means unthinkable."

Promoting this "third alternative" became Orwell's primary goal.

To see Orwell's two celebrated books in perspective, it is necessary to review his entire career. The phase of "political writing" between 1937 and 1950 is particularly crucial. *Animal Farm* and *1984* are distillates of a complex, energetic effort to urge socialist democracy as an alternative to capitalism and oligarchical collectivism.

Coming Up For Air

Victor Serge beautifully summarizes the qualities needed to "see clearly":

"To my mind it is a question less of exalted intelligence than of good sense, goodwill, and a certain courage. One must rise above pressures to close one's eyes, a temptation which fear inspires in us. A French essayist has said: 'What is terrible when you seek the truth is that you find it.' You find it, and then you are no longer free to accept fashionable clichés."

So it was with Orwell in the pre-war period. Fortunately, the ILP was still a sanctuary for revolutionary democratic sentiments. At this time there were 4000 ILP members.

Less than two weeks after joining the ILP, Orwell's "Why I Join" ran in the 24 June 1938 issue of the weekly party paper, *New Leader*. "The only régime which, in the long run, will dare to permit freedom of speech is a Socialist régime."

Orwell argued that, in the short run, all existing systems give political power to the small groups which run production, and that this power centralization was growing more pronounced.

In the impending European war, Orwell feared that "war necessity" would give rulers everywhere a pretext to pulverize labor and socialist opposition, just as in Spain.

To help prevent this, Orwell shared platforms with exiled POUM speakers, ILP leaders Brockway and Maxton, and George Padmore, founder of Pan-Africanism. He also wrote.

Orwell was not buoyantly optimistic. Far from it. "It may be just as possible to produce a breed of men who do not wish for liberty as to produce a breed of hornless cows. The Inquisition failed, but then the Inquisition lacked the resources of the modern state. Mass suggestion is a new invention . . ."

The specter of *1984* was visible on the horizon. Also, Orwell knew how weak worker solidarity was internationally: "The working-class of the world has regarded the Spanish war with detachment. Tens of thousands of individuals came to fight, but tens of millions remained apathetic." Solidarity between European and non-European workers was even weaker.

Still, Orwell remained cautiously hopeful. The prospect of co-operation between the middle-class and the working-class seemed bright as the persisting depression plunged salaried "middling elements" closer to the proles. Orwell criticized Fenner Brockway for being "too much dominated by the concept of a 'proletarian' as a manual laborer. In all western countries there now exists a huge middle-class whose interests are identical with those of the proletariat." Orwell's view was that pro-capitalist sentiment among salaried employees "is partly due to the tactlessness of Socialist propaganda."

With improved strategy and tact, Orwell believed that socialists *can* win middle sectors to their side; and that this *must* happen, if a critical revolutionary mass is to be attained. Concerned with the popular psychology necessary for effective political communication, Orwell penned a series of superb essays. "The Art of Donald McGill" is perhaps the most pertinent at this point.

Orwell finds McGill postcards to be a mirror for the "big public," which Orwell pictures as genial, unpretending, democratic, and self-reliant. The twin maladies of the age, power-worship and puritanism, are normally "alien" to most citizens. The danger to liberty lies not with the life-affirming big public, but with bureaucrats, capitalists, and rootless intellectuals.

Donald McGill was a genial master of cheerfully racy postcard cartoons (of which Orwell was very fond):

BY GEORGE, 'E'S DUCKY!

"Their whole meaning and virtue is in their unredeemed lowness. The slightest hint of 'higher' influence would ruin them utterly. They stand for the music-hall view of life, where marriage is a comic disaster, where the rent is always behind, the lawyer always a crook; where newlyweds make fools of themselves on hideous beds, and drunken red-nosed husbands roll home at four in the morning to meet grim-faced wives."

Just two kinds of people exist in McGill's world: the attractive young, and fat 'old marrieds.' All are motivated by lust, laziness, greed, cowardice, etc. McGill's tone, however, is hardly censorious. Frailties are winked at.

The wide popularity of this music-hall spirit shows that the big public is far from puritanical. People "want to be good, but not too good, and not quite all the time."

This leads Orwell to a formulation of real importance for him: "If you look into your own mind, which are you, Don Quixote or Sancho Panza? Almost certainly you are both. There is one part of you that wishes to be a hero or a saint, but another part of you is a little fat man who sees very clearly the advantages of staying alive with a whole skin."

The pressures of the work world force people to assume a Don Quixote posture. But inside, Sancho Panza rebels.

Moments of stolen pleasure as Sancho Panza compensate for the "faultless discipline" required to work hard, pay taxes, and maintain a family. (And business, of course, is happiest when "wicked pleasures" are not stolen, but *purchased.)*

Non-puritanical in its Sancho Panza mood, the big public may yet decide to act with Quixote resolve to genuinely satisfy the needs which production for profit leaves unfulfilled. Here lies a revolutionary motive.

Orwell is also encouraged by public freedom from malice. "One of the basic folk-tales of the English-speaking peoples is Jack the Giant-Killer—the little man against the big man. Mickey Mouse, Popeye the Sailor, and Charlie Chaplin are all essentially the same figure." Symbolized is "not merely a hatred of bullying, but a tendency to support the weaker side merely because it is weaker."

This popular sympathy for the underdog—seldom shared, Orwell feels, by modern intellectuals—can be mobilized for radical purposes . . .

This is Orwell's hope. It received early expression in Orwell's first 'political novel,' *Coming Up For Air* (1939).

Modified, this hope reappears in most later writings too.

Coming Up For Air is a remarkable book, one of Orwell's best. It is also probably the least well-known of his novels.

Synthesized in this book are virtually all the characteristic Orwellian themes: the plight of the shabby-genteel, the tyranny of the money-god, the entrapment of "the little man," the approach of war and totalitarianism, the psychology of servitude. Every previous book is echoed here, and every later book is prefigured.

Coming Up For Air is clearly intended to speak directly to the dispossessed middle-class. It starts where *Homage to Catalonia* stopped—in the London of "men in bowler hats and pigeons in Trafalgar Square, red buses and blue policemen—all sleeping the deep, deep sleep of England, from which I sometimes fear that we shall never wake till we are jerked out of it by the roar of bombs."

Hoping to waken as many people as possible before the bombs fall, Orwell reiterates again and again that the hour is late—that war looms three years, two years, one year away.

If it seems that Orwell wildly overestimated the potential impact of a minor novel by an obscure novelist, it pays to recall the later success of *Animal Farm* and *1984*. Evidently, Orwell's faith in the written word was not altogether misplaced. But the power of political writing is *problematic*. Neither *Animal Farm* nor *1984* had the impact Orwell expected. *Coming Up For Air*, meanwhile, was overlooked completely.

This is partly because Orwell's plot here is minimal. Never has a call to action been so filled with inaction. Nothing happens, except a brief, futile effort to escape history by fleeing into the past.

Orwell's supposition is that the "proles" are radically humanist, but that "middling blokes" like Flying Salamander Insurance salesman George Bowling are question marks. The radicalism of the protean "middle-class"—the contested middle, the swing vote—is in doubt.

The George Bowlings of the world must be *convinced* that the only alternative to war and dictatorship is collaboration with the working-class—to build a free society of equals.

With a brooding awareness of impending horrors, George Bowling seems ripe for radicalism. *Coming Up For Air*— reminiscent of "Wells watered down"—is intended to imply a left alternative for people like him. Says Bowling at one point: "Now and again you strike a book which is exactly at the mental level you've reached. One like that was H. G. Wells' *The History of Mr. Polly.*" Orwell aims for similar impact.

Who did Orwell hope to reach? Narrator Bowling is "slightly bookish" but otherwise "a typical middle-aged bloke, with about five quid a week" and a house in suburban West Bletchley. The son of Samuel Bowling, corn merchant, George Bowling is born the same year as John Flory (in 1893). While his father is slowly bankrupted by a giant food combine, George fishes avidly, studies moderately, and becomes a white-aproned grocer's assistant.

Injured slightly in the war in 1916, George is granted a pension big
enough to give him career options. He becomes an insurance salesman, marries into an Anglo-Indian family, turns fat overnight *à la*
Donald McGill (emerging as a life-sized Sancho Panza, "Fatty"
Bowling), and settles down "respectably" with a finicky wife and
two restless kids.

In typical Orwell fashion, Bowling is gifted with sales talent ("swind-
ling, I admit"). He concedes the paradox of his debt-slave existence:
"Merely because of the illusion that we own our houses—actually,
we're all in the middle of payments and eaten up with ghastly fear that
we might not finish them—we poor saps are all Tories, yes-men, and
bumsuckers.

Coming Up For Air shows the social descent of the shabby-genteel.
Samuel Bowling's bankruptcy is emblematic of the decay of the
shopkeeping class. George Bowling, meanwhile, is the quintessential
salaried employee—with an all-too-limited salary. Others in the
same leaky boat include a roll-call from Orwell's previous books:
Miss Minns, an unmarried 38-year-old clergyman's daughter just
scraping by; Anglo-Indian in-laws from the "poverty-stricken
officer-shareholder class;" bank clerks; etc.

The inspiration for *Coming Up For Air* came largely from Henry
Miller. Dismissed by many for writing about sexual matters with utter
frankness, "Miller is," according to Orwell, "simply a hardboiled
person talking about life, an ordinary American businessman with
intellectual courage and a gift for words." George Bowling, too, is an
ordinary articulate businessman

Henry Miller

Henry Miller exemplifies a completely passive outlook, "the viewpoint of a man who believes the world-process to be outside his control." This allows Miller "to get nearer to the ordinary man than is possible for more activist writers, since the ordinary man is also passive. Against major events, he is as helpless as against the elements. Far from trying to influence the future, he simply lies down and lets things happen to him.

Miller's "ordinary man" is "neither the manual worker nor the suburban householder," but the rootless adventurer. Orwell's candidate is the suburban householder: as passive as a snail, but alive to the future.

Coming Up For Air tries to frustrate the reader. Bowling's fatalism is a challenge. In effect, the reader is asked: Would you act differently? Bowling effectively lists the constraints on action:

> In the present, debt-slaves "quake and shiver, every one of them with the boss twisting his tail and the wife riding him like the nightmare and the kids sucking his blood like leeches." (This is the resentment underlying McGill-type humor.)

In the future, the boss will be even more terrifying—a dictator of a new type, "half-gangster, half-gramophone."

(Ezra Pound affectionately called Mussolini ''the
Boss.'' Mussolini had coined the term 'totalitarianism' to describe Fascist power.)

Feeling afflicted with near-clairvoyance—''it felt as if I'd
got x-rays in my eyes and could see the skeletons
walking''—George makes a quiet, desperate return to
Lower Binfield in an effort to recapture childhood serenity.
''Fear is our element. We swim in it.'' George decides to
come up for air.

Fishing, he thinks; he'll go fishing. ''Fishing is the opposite of war . . . . The very idea of sitting all day under a
willow tree beside a quiet pool belongs to the time before
the war, before bombers, before Hitler.'' (For Orwell,
fishing is also a sexual metaphor.)

But the Lower Bin-
field of rusting mem-
ory no longer exists.
George finds that his
beloved fishing pond
is now a rubbish
dump. The former
village is a booming
manufacturing town.
The gleaming factory
makes bombs.

"Funny. It was exactly to escape the thought of war that I'd come here. But how could I escape? War's in the air we breathe. The old life's finished. There's no way back to Lower Binfield; you can't put Jonah back into the whale."

This returns us to Henry Miller, who Orwell had compared to the Biblical Jonah. Hiding inside the whale ("simply a bigger womb") is no longer possible, Orwell tells Miller. In a world of "concentration camps, aeroplanes, machine-guns, putsches, purges, spies," etc., one either surrenders or resists. Miller's attitude is tantamount to surrender.

Is this also George Bowling's attitude? No and yes—hence, the tension in *Coming Up For Air*.

Visions of 1984-style repression haunt Bowling.

"War! It's coming soon, that's certain. 1941, they say. The bombs, the streamlined bullets. But it wasn't the war that matters, it's the after-war. The world we're entering, the Hate-world, Slogan-world. Colored shirts, barbed wire. Secret cells where electric lights burn night and day; detectives watching you sleep. And posters with enormous faces, huge crowds cheering wildly for the Leader while underneath, they hate him violently."

Bowling sees a rising curve of bully-worship. Like Reich, he sees that people in a chaotic world react to powerlessness and insecurity with a wish for power and security. This expresses itself in two main forms—either in the wish to be a boss, or in identification with a boss. Frequently, boss-worship is tinged with elements of sexual sadism.

The *alternative* to boss-worship is socialist humanism. For its diffusion, this requires widespread foresight into the dangers of war and the Hate-World. But foresight does not necessarily lead to resistance. Take George Bowling, for example . . .

At his most Orwell-like, Bowling presents a choice: "There's no escape. Fight the Hate-World, pretend not to notice, or grab your wrench and do a bit of face-smashing yourself. But there's no way out."

All society seems to conspire against resistance. Driving to Lower Binfield Bowling is overcome by a feeling that he's being pursued: "It was as if a huge army were streaming up the road behind me. I seemed to see them in my mind's eye. Hilda in front, of course, with the kids tagging after her, and the Flying Salamander higher-ups in their Rolls-Royces. And all the people you've never seen but who rule your destiny: Scotland Yard, the Bank of England, Hitler and Stalin on a bicycle, Mussolini, the Pope—they were all after me. It's queer. The impression was so strong that I actually took a peep."

This reveals something real. If you stray from the path of least resistance, numberless forces can make life difficult for you, from the State to your family.

In a McGill-like way, Bowling feels that his wife Hilda hems him in. Hilda "does everything for negative reasons; when she makes a cake she's not thinking about the cake, only about how to save butter and eggs."

"She's got this feeling that you *ought* to be perpetually working yourself up into a stew about lack of money. 'But, George! You don't seem to *realize!* We've simply got no money at all! It's very *serious!*'"

Bowling's entrapment, however, is not Hilda's fault. It may be easy
to sympathize with poor George in this cartoon-like scene from his
marriage, but turn the equation around. Poor Fatty Bowling feels
duty bound to stew over the pre-war crisis. His entire narrative
reduces to the plaintive cry: ''But people! You don't seem to
realize! It's very *serious!''* Why should Hilda or anyone else take
such a warning seriously when George isn't prepared to *do* something about it? At least Hilda's money woes are more-or-less
manageable. Why fret over an impending catastrophe about which
it seems that nothing can or will be done?

War and Revolution

The 1939 Orwell/Bowling answer is that something can and very likely will be done. Bowling simulates rhetorical resignation:

"The future! What's the future got to do with chaps like you and me? Holding down our jobs—that's our future. As for Hilda, even when the bombs are dropping she'll still be thinking about the price of butter."

However, beneath this seeming passivity, both Georges clearly expect the coming war to provoke action.

"If the war didn't kill you it was bound to start you thinking.
  People who normally were about as likely to think for themselves as
  a suet pudding were turned into Bolshies by the last war."
  Bowling's ultimate paralysis is a symbolic incitement to resistance.

Not until post-war did Orwell finally concede that Hilda might *really* stay fixated on the price of butter: "Never would I have prophesied that we could go through nearly six years of war without arriving at either Socialism or Fascism. I don't know whether this semi-anesthesia in which the British people contrive to live is a sign of decadence or a kind of instinctive wisdom."

Anticipating pre-war upheaval, Orwell prepared for direct action. He wrote to Herbert Read: "I believe it is vitally necessary to start organizing for illegal anti-war activities. Otherwise we may find ourselves absolutely helpless when war or the pre-war fascising processes begin."

As a start, Orwell proposed the purchase of a printing press for clandestine publishing (perhaps in conjunction with anti-war philosopher Bertrand Russell).

Orwell held the ILP view that "capitalist-imperialist wars" are utterly indefensible, since all contending parties seek only power and profit. War preparations allow the capitalist class to impose austerity on workers ("guns, not butter").

Orwell dismissed the complacent assumption that "the huge British and French empires—in essence nothing but mechanisms for exploiting colored labor"—merited defense against Hitler and Mussolini. "How can we 'fight Fascism' except by bolstering up a far vaster injustice? For of course it *is* vaster. What we always forget is that the overwhelming bulk of the British proletariat does not live in Britain, but in Asia and Africa. It is not in Hitler's power to make a penny a normal hourly wage; it is perfectly normal in India . . ."

When the long-awaited war finally came, however, Orwell performed an about-face. Taking the war as a given, Orwell decided that it would be an unmitigated catastrophe if Fascism were to prevail. Fascism would terrorize workers and paralyze the struggle for socialism. For this reason alone—along the line of arguments by Marx and the Bolsheviks in favor of capitalist democracy rather than autocracy—Orwell felt that the war must be won. His views had sharply shifted:

"The feeling of all true patriots and all true socialists is at bottom reducible to the 'Trotskyist' slogan: 'The war and the revolution are inseparable.' We cannot beat Hitler without passing through revolution, nor consolidate our revolution without beating Hitler." Both of these last two provisos were seriously intended by Orwell . . .

Part of this seemed clearly true: a Nazi victory over England would hurt the English working-class and limit the chance of revolution. But Orwell's corollary claim, that a Nazi defeat could be won only by a revolutionary England, was far shakier. Orwell overestimated public volatility, while underestimating the fighting capacity of the British ruling-class.

About the ruling-class. Orwell considered the English moneyed class too sympathetic to Fascism to fight it effectively: "How can these people possibly rouse the nation against *Fascism* when they themselves are subjectively pro-Fascist and were buttering up Mussolini till almost the moment when Italy entered the war?" He quoted Churchill's 1927 toast to Mussolini: "If I had been an Italian I am sure I should have been whole-heartedly with you in your triumphant struggle against the bestial appetites and passions of Leninism."

Yes, English businessmen "always have been on Hitler's side" against the working-class; but no

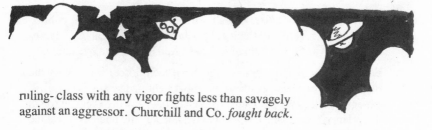

ruling-class with any vigor fights less than savagely against an aggressor. Churchill and Co. *fought back*.

A second error was the view that private capitalism is too weak to compete with "totalitarianism." Impressed by the speed of German rearmament, Orwell felt that Nazi state-capitalism had eclipsed the military-economic capacity of less centralized capitalism. Russia too seemed capable of faster and more efficient militarization. This was simply wrong. Like James Burnham and Max Schachtman, Orwell felt that private capitalism was fated for extinction. The question, they thought, was whether it would be replaced by statist or by democratic collectivism.

At this stage, Orwell considered Nazism far worse than Stalinism. But both are, for Orwell, "totalitarian." An after-war with either dominant would be a nightmare. The war offered a golden opportunity to replace capitalism not with totalitarianism, but with revolutionary democracy. This was Orwell's hope.

About the working-class. Orwell seriously misjudged the big public, too. A definite leftward trend did produce a post-war Labour government, but was far too mild to justify Orwell's inflated expectations.

Whether Orwell's rosy hopes might have been closer to the mark if the ruling-class had been as irresolute about fighting the war as Orwell expected will never be known. But Orwell—viewing events through the prism of the Spanish war—unquestionably did underestimate the very real nationalism and reformism of the big public.

yril Connolly captures something of Orwell's mood at this time: "He had seen it nearly happen in Spain, and now it seemed inevitable. This time the gamble must come off, *Revolution or Disaster*. A series of defeats would topple the British ruling class; in the nick of time the People would kick them out and take control, snatching victory at the last moment."

Sub rosa, Orwell's patriotism was emotional. In 1940 he reported a dream in which, suddenly, he knew that he could never accept an English defeat. In his heart of hearts, Orwell was a patriot.

Careful not to make invidious comparisons with other nations—saying, *e.g.,* that *Fascism* (not Germany) is the central enemy—Orwell nevertheless showers praise on England: "The beer is bitterer, the coins are heavier, the grass is greener . . . . Above all, it is *your* civilization, it is *you.* The suet puddings and the red pillar-boxes have entered into your soul."

Orwell later disavowed *The Lion and the Unicorn,* but it clearly reflected his war-time feelings.

Eileen and George moved to London to be closer to the war. Orwell tried to enlist in the army but was turned down; Eileen's brother Laurence was killed in France; Georges Kopp, now Eileen's brother-in-law, joined the French Resistance.

Eager to see action, Orwell joined the Home Guard—a volunteer militia which he hoped would become a revolutionary force. "Here were a million men springing, as it were, out of the ground, asking for arms to defend their country against a possible invader and organizing themselves into a military body almost without direction from above. It apparently did not occur to most Socialists that the political color of such a force, compelled by the circumstances of the time to organize itself independently, would be determined by the people who were in it." Orwell remained in the Home Guard for three years.

In 1941 Orwell accepted a B.B.C. position as Talks Producer for war broadcasts to India. Asked to do this because he was popular in India as an anti-imperialist, Orwell consented with the proviso that he would not accept censorship. For two years, Orwell broadcasted to India. The pressure and futility of this work left him feeling like a "sucked orange." Few Indians had radios, and Orwell worked too rapidly to satisfy his perfectionist impulses.

Sometimes, too, Orwell found himself slanting the news like a real propagandist. The only bright spot was the opportunity to involve other writers in the work. Dylan Thomas, E. M. Forster, Stevie Smith, T. S. Eliot, William Empson, and George Woodcock were among Orwell's collaborators in this period.

In November 1943, Orwell became the Literary Editor of
the socialist *Tribune,* for which he wrote the popular "As I
Please" column. In the same month Orwell started a
book he had long planned: *Animal Farm,* which he completed in February 1944.

Animal Farm was the only one of Orwell's books with which
he was entirely pleased. A parable of the Russian Revolution
and its subsequent betrayal, *Animal Farm* was written to
counter the widespread view that Socialism = Stalinism.
Russia, as a war ally, was very popular in England, and
Orwell hoped to immunize readers against potential disillu-
sionment with socialism when Russian infamies came to light.

"Russian behavior is not worse than that of capitalist governments. The point is the effect of the Russian myth on the
Socialist movement *here.* Nothing had contributed so much
to the corruption of the original idea of Socialism as the belief
that Russia is a Socialist country.

The plot of *Animal Farm* was not especially original. Kipling
had written a story in the 1890's about "a yellow horse" who
tried to rouse Vermont farm animals against "the Oppressor " man, and as recently as 1941 an excellent, funny
children's book *(Freddy and the Ignormus* by Walter
Brooks) had recounted a tale of the "First Animal Republic." But Orwell's handling of his material was entirely
original.

Animal Farm is a precise, balanced allegory superb-
ly crafted. It can be read either as a strictly political
document, or, by children, as an innocent animal
story. Eileen was particularly fond of this book, and helped
plan it.

Animal Farm

The central concept of *Animal Farm* is simple. Orwell saw a little boy in Wallington ''whipping a huge carthorse along a narrow path. It struck me that if only such animals became aware of their strength we should have no power over them, and that men exploit animals in much the same way as the rich exploit the proletariat.''

A prize boar on the Jones Farm, old Major, arrives at just this insight, ''Marx's theory from the animals' point of view,'' which he explains to his fellow animals. In accents reminiscent of Hobbes, old Major tells of a life ''miserable, laborious, and short.''

''We are born, we are given just so much food as will keep the breath in our bodies, and those of us who are capable of it are forced to work to the last atom of our strength; and the very instant that our usefulness has come to an end we are slaughtered with hideous cruelty. No animal in England is free.''

"Is this simply a part of the order of nature? Is it because this land of ours is so poor that it cannot afford a decent life to those who dwell upon it? No, comrades, a thousand times no!"

Old Major dies, but not before his message takes root. Snowball, Napoleon, and other young boars begin proselytizing for revolution. The plowhorses, Boxer and Clover, the goat, Muriel, and other animals are won over.

'Animalist' doctrine spreads quickly, and one day, when Mr. Jones leaves the farm, the animals establish control.

When Jones and his neighbors try to recapture the farm with firearms, Snowball leads a successful resistance.

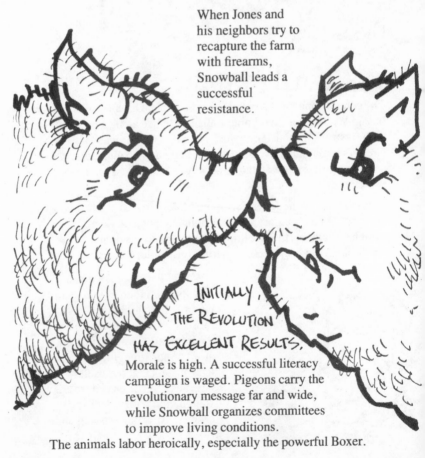

INITIALLY, THE REVOLUTION HAS EXCELLENT RESULTS.

Morale is high. A successful literacy campaign is waged. Pigeons carry the revolutionary message far and wide, while Snowball organizes committees to improve living conditions.
The animals labor heroically, especially the powerful Boxer.

Just as the future begins to look really bright—Snowball devises a windmill which will permit work reductions—Napoleon springs a *coup d'etat*. Snarling dogs reared from birth by Napoleon chase Snowball away.

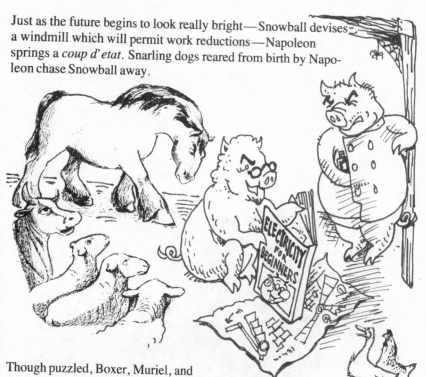

Though puzzled, Boxer, Muriel, and the other animals develop implicit faith in "our leader, Comrade Napoleon." "Napoleon is always right," says Boxer. Only the wise old donkey, Benjamin, Boxer's loyal friend, is skeptical. (Orwell's friends Celia Kirwan and Mamaine Koestler started calling Orwell "Donkey George" after reading *Animal Farm*.)

Methodically, every trace of equality is stripped away as Napoleon and his fellow pigs turn into a ruling caste. Animalist doctrine is transformed: by inspired doublethink, "All animals are equal" becomes "All animals are equal, but some animals are more equal than others." History is rewritten. Boxer, crippled by overwork, is shipped to the glue factory. Dissidents are killed. Memories of the revolution grow dim.

Finally, Napoleon and Co. acquire human characteristics and make peace with the neighboring farmers. Farmer Pilkington jokes: "If you have your lower animals to contend with, we have our lower classes!"

Vintage Orwell, *Animal Farm* has stunning virtues. The admirably clear prose and adept story-telling are legendary. Politically and historically the parable is quite accurate.

Napoleon/Stalin's rise to power is lucidly chronicled, with few important events omitted. Snowball—a composite of Lenin and Trotsky—is portrayed as a contradictory figure, not fully democratic *(e.g.,* sanctioning extra apples and milk for pigs), but revolutionary and popular.

In other writings Orwell argues that neither Lenin nor Trotsky can be exempted from criticism of Stalin. This is less subtle than the position taken in *Animal Farm.*

Lenin and Trotsky without question share responsibility for the limitation of democracy in Soviet Russia. Both abused power.

But Lenin and Trotsky were *liberators* as well as dictators, with an ultimate tendency that remains uncertain. At different times, they embodied different principles.

Finally, Orwell gives no credence to the myth that Marx, like Stalin, was an oligarchical collectivist. Old Major's revolutionary speech ends with the injunction, "Above all, no animal must ever tyrannize over his own kind. Weak or strong, clever or simple, we are all brothers. All animals are equal."

Orwell's tilt in favor of socialism seems plain. He assails Stalinism but shows Socialism to be a welcome change from oppression (if vulnerable to betrayal). This is *not,* however, how *Animal Farm* is usually read. Orwell is sabotaged by the very prejudice he tries to undermine. Criticizing Stalinism, he appears to criticize Socialism.

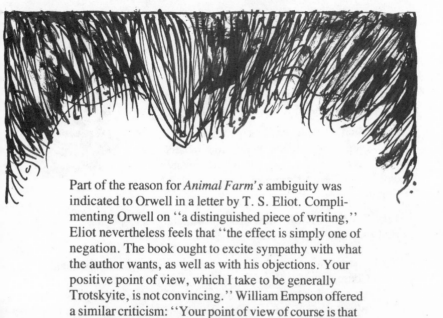

Part of the reason for *Animal Farm's* ambiguity was indicated to Orwell in a letter by T. S. Eliot. Complimenting Orwell on "a distinguished piece of writing," Eliot nevertheless feels that "the effect is simply one of negation. The book ought to excite sympathy with what the author wants, as well as with his objections. Your positive point of view, which I take to be generally Trotskyite, is not convincing." William Empson offered a similar criticism: "Your point of view of course is that the animals ought to have gone on sharing Animal Farm. But your metaphor—the intellectual superiority of the pigs—suggests that the Russian revolution was a pathetically impossible effort to defy nature. You must expect to be 'misunderstood' about this book on a large scale."

Power-Worship

In a series of essays transitional between *Animal Farm* (1943) and *1984* (1949), Orwell takes a stance very close to that of such radical psychoanalysts as Wilhelm Reich and Erich Fromm.

Like Reich, Orwell analyzes the "mass psychology" of Fascism, which both writers define as authoritarianism tinged with sexual sadism—in Orwell's phrase, "power-worship."

Like Fromm, Orwell is preoccupied with the flight from freedom into submission.

The question for all such thinkers is why people accept tyranny. Coercion and fear play a part, but consent and conformism are also involved. Some of the oppressed embrace their oppression. Why? Not a psychoanalyst, Orwell analyzes power-worship in art, politics, and popular culture . . .

WONDERFUL COMPLETE SCHOOL STORY and FREE PHOTO-PLATE *INSIDE.*

Th **MAGNET** 2°

In "Boys' Weeklies," written shortly after George Bowling tried to surface in the vanished air of childhood memories, Orwell returns to the same fading past for a comparison of old and new boys' magazines.

Gem and *Magnet* had been the leading 'penny dreadfuls' for decades. Both magazines were the product of a single writer, Frank Richards, and both created fantasy-worlds of adventure and misadventure among boy heroes at great public schools resembling Eton.

Frank Richards

Although conservative in the most old-fashioned way, *Gem* and *Magnet* were innocent. The boy heroes personified every "public school" virtue—sportsmanship, perseverance, fair-play. Inciting to "wealth-fantasy" rather than violence-fantasy, *Gem* and *Magnet* were snobbish but light-hearted.

Striking contrast is provided by the boys' weeklies of the late thirties. Though mild by later standards, the new favorites *(Thriller, Hotspur)* were sensationalist and harsh compared to earlier ones. A taste for exotic violence and danger had emerged.

Crash ! "Yoo-hoop !" roared Bunter. "Wow ! Oh crikey ! My jaw's broken ! Ow ! Wow !" "What is this ?" thundered Mr. Quelch. "I will keep order in this class ! Who threw that book ? Was it you, Vernon-Smith ?" The Bounder glared.

Orwell sees a parallel change in grown-up literature. Comparing two crime stories "which play the limelight on the criminal rather than the policeman," Orwell finds an "immense difference in moral atmosphere." *Raffles*, the raffish gentleman burglar of 1900, is a "public school man gone astray." Though "a cad," Raffles is not dishonorable.

No Orchids for Miss Blandish, by contrast, is "aimed at the power instinct." "A brilliant piece of writing, with hardly a wasted word or a jarring note anywhere," this 1939 story brims with "cruelty and sexual perversion."

"*No Orchids* takes for granted the most complete corruption and self-seeking as the norm of human behavior. Such things as affection, friendship, good nature or even ordinary politeness simply do not enter. Nor, to any great extent, does normal sexuality. Ultimately only one motive is at work: the pursuit of power."

Sadism is on the rise in popular culture, Orwell feels; if Jack the Giant-Kiler was the prototypical hero of old, perhaps he should be renamed "Jack the Dwarf-Killer" for modern consumption.

Elsewhere, Orwell finds a similar trend: in violent public sports, in widespread fascination with the police, and in impersonal murder. "Emancipation," he says ironically, "is complete. Freud and Machiavelli have reached the outer suburbs."

Sigmund Freud

THANX TO LAURA BENNETTS for THESE SUBLIMINALS!

And not just the suburbs. The urban *literati* are tarred with the same brush—a brush wielded, in one instance, by surrealist painter Salvador Dali.

In Dali's autobiography Orwell finds "a direct, unmistakable assault on life, sanity, and decency." Dali revels in sadism, narcissism, and death-worship. His art is also morbid.

Dali's perversity is popular, Orwell feels, in part due to the decline of humanist sensibilities. But this works both ways. Orwell also feels that, for Dali, perversity is a *gimmick* calculated to appeal to post-humanist tastes. Fundamentally, Orwell feels Dali is skilled but unoriginal: "Picturesqueness keeps breaking in. Take away the skulls, ants, lobsters, and telephones, and you are back in the fairytale illustrator's world."

Sadism sells paintings . . .

Orwell's main concern was now "a huge subject whose edges have barely been scratched: the interconnection between sadism, masochism, success-worship, power-worship, nationalism, and totalitarianism."

Reich, Fromm, and others had ventured into this *terra incognita:* Orwell followed. In "Notes on Nationalism" (1945), Orwell mapped "the lunatic habit of identifying oneself with large power units"—nations, empires, churches, etc.

NATIONAL UNION OF JOURNALISTS

7 John Street, Bedford Row, London, W.C.I
'Phone :   Telegrams :
HOLborn 2258   Natujay Holb, London

This is to certify that

Mr. GEORGE ORWELL

of The Tribune

is a member of the   Γ . Ŧ P .
Branch of the National Union of Journalists.

Leslie R. Aldous   Branch Sec.

This habit is crucial. No "large power unit" is powerful without zealous subjects. Hence, the importance of understanding zealots. To start, Orwell looks into "the habit of classifying whole populations of millions or tens of millions as 'good' or 'bad'." The worst consequence of this is a failure to accept moral responsibility for people outside the "good" nation. It may, Orwell agrees, be perfectly legitimate to fight a collective enemy bitterly; but people are enemies not by virtue of inherent national traits. An exploiting group should be resisted, but it is the *exploitation,* not the group, which is fundamentally in question. Your enemies are human, too.

Positive nationalism—"My country, right or wrong"—is supplemented by negative nationalism ("the Russians are to blame"). In either form, nationalism is an excuse for aggression. Patriotism, by contrast, is defensive. Where patriotism rests on love for a group, nationalism rests on love for group *power*.

Infected by nationalism, "the most intelligent people seem capable of holding schizophrenic beliefs." They disregard facts, evade questions, embrace false rumors, and accept the distortion of history.

As the war ended Orwell entered the final phase of his life. *Animal Farm* was published in 1945 to great acclaim. The Blairs adopted a baby (Richard) in 1944. With Koestler and others, Orwell helped organize a human rights group prefiguring Amnesty International.

Then, with fame and fortune immi nent, Orwell's life began to unravel.

While in Germany as a war correspondent in early 1945, Orwell learned of Eileen's death during what they had imagined would be minor surgery. His health worsened drastically.

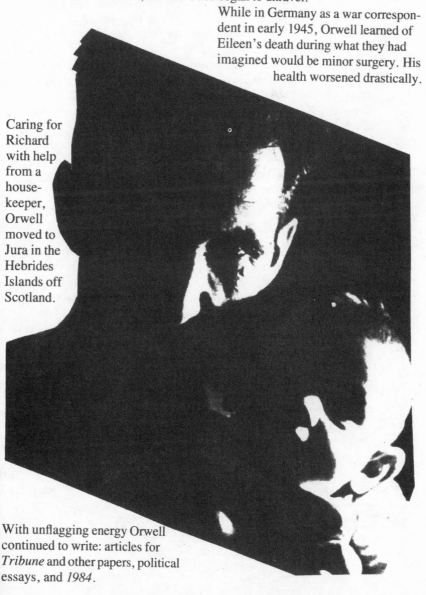

Caring for Richard with help from a house-keeper, Orwell moved to Jura in the Hebrides Islands off Scotland.

With unflagging energy Orwell continued to write: articles for *Tribune* and other papers, political essays, and *1984*.

Problems of nationalism and power-worship remained central to Orwell's post-war thinking. *1984* is the final fruit of a lifelong concern with liberty and equality.

The political specifics of *1984* derive largely from several key debates. With Serge, Borkenau, James, Koestler *et al.*, Orwell agreed that Soviet Russia is non-socialist. Fine—but what does this imply? Is socialism likely to succeed oligarchical collectivism in Russia?

Probably the greatest single influence on Orwell in this period was James Burnham, a particularly bold and erratic ex-Trotskyist. In 1940 Burnham had published *The Managerial Revolution*—a book clearly indebted to Trotsky's *The Revolution Betrayed*, but with a non-socialist slant. Burnham agreed with Orwell, Max Schachtman, and others that private capitalism is doomed—it is, he felt, too anarchic to compete with "managerial" regimes *à la* Germany, Italy, and Russia. *But Burnham argued that socialism will never be a viable alternative*. Oligarchical collectivism is the future—period.

Orwell sharply disagreed:

"The real question is not whether the people who wipe their boots on us during the next fifty years are to be called managers, bureaucrats, or politicians; the question is whether capitalism, now obviously doomed, is to give way to oligarchy or true democracy."

Heir to Machiavelli, Burnham argued that (in the language of the sociologist Michels) there is an "iron law of oligarchy." With sociologist Vilfredo Pareto, Burnham insisted that democracy is a mirage; the "circulation of elites" is all history offers.

"As an interpretation of what is *happening*, Burnham's theory is extremely plausible." Orwell was particularly impressed by Burnham's contention that the globe is dividing into three great unconquerable power blocs, each permanently at odds with the others and internally undemocratic.

Orwell disagreed, however, that this is inevitable.

James Burnham

Yes, post-capitalist regimes so far have not been socialist "in any sense of the word which would have been accepted by Marx or Lenin or William Morris, or, indeed, by any leading socialist prior to about 1930." But Burnham's position is far too total. O'Brien, the Inquisitor in *1984*, sounds just like Burnham. (And note, too, the resemblance of Burnham's view to the outlook in *No Orchids for Miss Blandish*):

"What Burnham is mainly concerned to show is that a democratic society has never existed and, so far as we can see, never will exist. Burnham does not deny that 'good' motives may operate in private life, but he maintains that politics consists of the struggle for power and nothing else. All talk about democracy, liberty, equality, fraternity; all revolutionary movements; all visions of Utopia or 'the classless society' or 'the Kingdom of Heaven on earth'; all these are humbug.

"In effect, humanity is divided into two classes: the greedy, hypocritical minority; and the brainless mob, whose destiny is always to be led or driven. And this beautiful pattern is to continue forever."

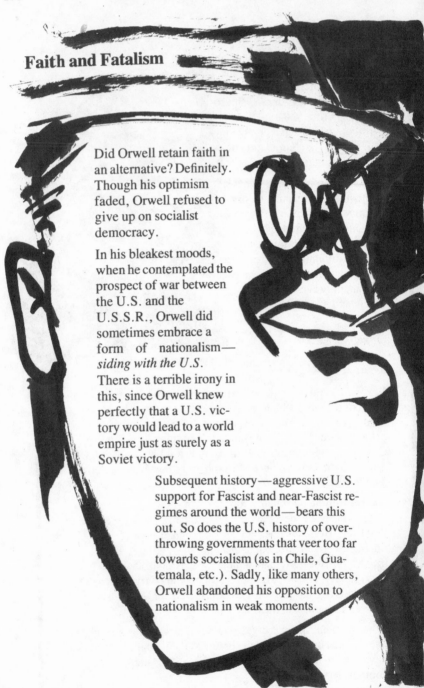

Faith and Fatalism

Did Orwell retain faith in an alternative? Definitely. Though his optimism faded, Orwell refused to give up on socialist democracy.

In his bleakest moods, when he contemplated the prospect of war between the U.S. and the U.S.S.R., Orwell did sometimes embrace a form of nationalism— *siding with the U.S.* There is a terrible irony in this, since Orwell knew perfectly that a U.S. victory would lead to a world empire just as surely as a Soviet victory.

Subsequent history—aggressive U.S. support for Fascist and near-Fascist regimes around the world—bears this out. So does the U.S. history of overthrowing governments that veer too far towards socialism (as in Chile, Guatemala, etc.). Sadly, like many others, Orwell abandoned his opposition to nationalism in weak moments.

Mainly, though, Orwell retained his vision of a liberated future. The preponderance of his energy went, as usual, to provoking ''the big public'' to see democratic collectivism as an alternative to oligarchy and the profit-motive.

Specifically, Orwell urged a Socialist United States of Europe. ''The only way I can imagine to avoid nuclear war or a spiralling arms race, either of which would spell an end to democracy, is by generating the spectacle of a community where people are relatively free and happy and where the main motive in life is not the pursuit of money or power.''

Europe seemed to pose the brightest hope since (at the time) ''perhaps half the skilled industrial workers of the world live here,'' and since European democratic traditions are reasonably powerful.

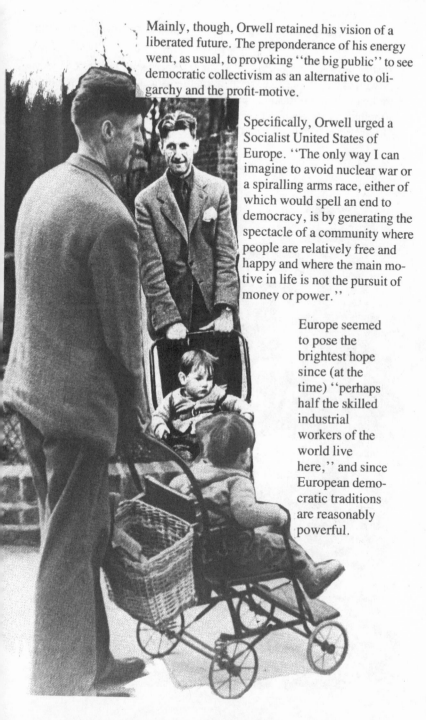

Let's turn, now, to *1984*. Here Orwell's opposition to power-worship and nationalism rises to a paradigmatic level.

Just as with *Animal Farm*, *1984* was an experiment. Described by Orwell as "a Utopia in the form of a naturalistic novel," *1984* is a link in the chain of political Utopias extending back to Thomas More and Jonathan Swift. Swift's masterpiece, *Gulliver's Travels*, was one of Orwell's favorite books, and it unmistakably influenced *1984*.

"Swift's greatest contribution to political thought is his extraordinarily clear prevision of the spy-haunted 'police State,' with its endless heresy hunts and treason trials, all really designed to neutralize popular discontent by changing it into war hysteria."

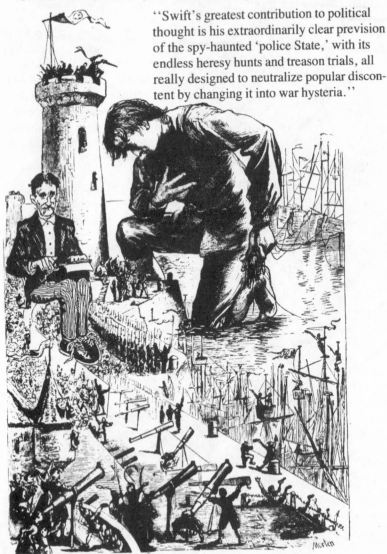

illiam Morris came much closer to Orwell in his seminal *News from Nowhere* (1891). The great early Marxist, however, painted a picture of sweetness and light, with just a brief nod to the harder realities from which Utopia emerged. (Utopia is Greek for "no-where.")

Utopia?

Twentieth-century "utopias" became considerably grimmer in tone, starting with Jack London and H. G. Wells. London's *The Iron Heel* (1909) was a stark, violent account of a Fascist-style regime of plutocratic Oligarchs opposed by working-class warriors. Wells, though best known for his visions of glittering Utopian cities, also wrote "negative utopias" showing future dangers. Orwell thought highly, in particular, of *When the Sleeper Wakes* (1899).

Another book which influenced Orwell was Yevgeny Zamyatin's *We* (1923). Zamyatin, an admirer of Wells, was a Russian engineer disillusioned by the 1917 revolution. He depicted a total police-state in which citizens live under constant surveillance in all-glass apartments. Virtually every movement is public. D-503, the hero, steps beyond the pale when he falls in love with I-330, a revolutionary.

After being captured by the authorities, D-503 is subjected to a "fantasiectomy" which kills his capacity for subversive thought.

Yevgeny Zamyatin

We was a major influence not only on *1984*, but on Aldous Huxley's celebrated *Brave New World* (1932), which portrays a far-distant future of hygienic hedonism where little Polly Trotsky and lovers Lenina Crowne and Bernard Marx are suffocated by soulless social engingeering. Huxley's specific inspirations were Henry Ford, the *Brave New World's* reigning deity, and John Broadus Watson, the pioneering psychological behaviorist; where Ford implemented the mass production of cars, Watson envisaged the mass production of pliant workers and consumers.

Huxley's vision of an evil future is mild compared to Orwell's. Where Orwell shows a regime founded on terror as well as psychological conditioning, Huxley contends that *hypnopedia* (the indoctrination of sleepers) would be sufficient by itself.

Also parallel to *1984* is the savagely brilliant *It Can't Happen Here* (1935) by Sinclair Lewis—a portrayal of Fascism coming to the U.S. draped in the flag.

Other influences include Koestler's *Darkness at Noon* (1940), stories by E. M. Forster, Cyril Connolly, and Robin Maugham, etc. Nabokov's *Bend Sinister* (1947) is so pedantically elephantine that we can accept at face value Nabokov's indignant protest that its similarities to *1984* are strictly superficial.

Sinclair Lewis

An anti-socialist reply to Orwell, *1985* (1978), was published by the catholic novelist Anthony Burgess, famous for *A Clockwork Orange*.

Composed mainly in 1948—"84" is just "48" transposed— *1984* was followed shortly afterwards by two similar works, Bradbury's *Fahrenheit 451* (1953), and Vonnegut's *Player Piano* (1952).

Nineteen Eighty-Four is a *tour de force*. The plot is slender, the characterization thin, the logic not altogether cohesive—and yet the book rings true. It makes its point.

Orwell was trying less to simulate a probable future than to "parody the implications of totalitarianism." To do this, it was necessary to streamline and caricature the future. Reduced to bare surreal bones, Orwell's chilling fantasy is only effective if the reader can be forced into a suspension of disbelief. For most readers *1984* achieves this effect.

O'Brien, the wise and benevolent torturer, is not a credible character. Reviewing *The Iron Heel*, Orwell had praised Jack London precisely for showing that no ruling group concedes its venality, even to itself; yet O'Brien is burdened with full awareness of his power-madness.

Winston Smith, who invites arrest and torture for the sake of a phantom rebellion, is a dessicated, dry-as-dust character.

Yet somehow Winston feels credible. So does O'Brien. For a few brief moments it seems plausible that society could be so extreme that subjects would be as vacant as Winston Smith, while rulers would be as lucidly demented as O'Brien.

PLOT STRUCTURE IS NOT WHAT MAKES 1984 EXCEPTIONAL.

Two minor civil servants in a gleaming high-tech dictatorship enter into an illicit love affair and decide to oppose the regime. They are captured, tortured, and broken.

Similar events have transpired in countless places in recent decades, from Mussolini's Italy to Pahlavi's Iran . . .

What makes *1984* exceptional is the extreme simplification of character which Orwell considers possible for an extremely authoritarian regime: the formation of "benevolent dictators" without benevolence and subjects without subjectivity . . .

Winston Smith is "weakly characterized" because he is genuinely weak; after a lifetime of rigorous conditioning, Winston is burnt-out. a mass of self-protective reflexes with no self to protect.

> When Winston's conditioning goes haywire, he flips from one extreme to another—winding up as self-conscious and active, but *not* self-protective. O'Brien, meanwhile, routinely oscillates between extremes. Supremely efficient, he is also madder than the Mad Hatter (shifting from cruel competence to Lewis Carroll *doublethink* in the twinkling of a rationalization).

> Julia, Winston's lover, goes through equally strange changes. And "the proles" are too silent to be believed, a big public of Sancho Panzas without a Don Quixote in sight . . . yet still, potentially (so Winston believes), a voice and force for revolution.

The electricity which powers the ruling system in *1984* can be called "anti-humanism": a mix of power-worship, repression, self-repression, and dictatorship which (Orwell felt) could turn people into walking two-dimensional caricatures. In *1984*, rulers and ruled alike are dehumanized: Party leaders rejoice in cruel power, while Party victims decline to semi-consciousness.

> *If Orwell can persuade us* that this is a plausible eventuality, given present trends, then his goal (provoking resistance) will have been half-achieved. But to be fully effective, Orwell's allegory must also define alternative possibilities . . . Here *1984* is highly problematic.

When O'Brien and Winston meet in the torture chamber, O'Brien openly avows the anti-humanism of Party motives. He makes no effort to justify Party rule in the self-seeking terms of Dostoyevsky's Grand Inquisitor, so ably reproduced in *Animal Farm* by Napoleon's mouthpiece, Squealer:

"Do not imagine, comrades, that leadership is a pleasure! On the contrary, it is a deep and heavy responsibility. No one believes more firmly than Comrade Napoleon that all animals are equal. He would be only too happy to let you make your decisions yourselves. But sometimes you might make the wrong decisions, and then where should we be?"

By contrast, O'Brien is brazen: "The Party seeks power entirely for its own sake. We are not interested in the good of others; we are interested solely in power. Power is tearing human minds to pieces and putting them together again in new shapes."

O'Brien's motive is two-fold: to revel in cruelty for its own sake, and to secure perfect, voluntary obedience. In *The Discourse of Voluntary Servitude* (1550), Étienne de La Boétie summarizes the latter principle in a way that pre-figures *Animal Farm* as well as *1984*:

"Men are like handsome race horses, who first bite the bit and later like it, and rearing under the saddle a while soon learn to enjoy displaying their harness and prance proudly beneath their trappings."

La Boétie deplored this; O'Brien exults in it; Winston and Julia prove it partly false.

Above all, O'Brien's Party seeks unre-
sisting compliance from its mass lower
bureaucracy, the so-called "Outer
Party." (Proles who show too much
talent are simply vaporized.) The
Outer Party is controlled by puritanical
behaviorist conditioning and police
surveillance.

Party scientists "study with extraordinary minuteness the meaning of facial
expressions, gestures, and tones of
voice." Even heartbeats are
monitored. The goal? "To discover,
against his will, what another human
being is thinking."

Newspeak, the Party language,
banishes troublesome words such as
"freedom" and "equality" altogether
to minimize the very *possibility* of im-
proper thoughts. Just as in Swift's evil
utopia, the goal here is "not merely to
make sure that people will think the
right thoughts, but actually to make
them *less conscious.*"

(Interestingly, when
Orwell wrote *1984* a
behaviorist effort to
purify language of
"metaphysical"
meanings was the

BIG BROT
IS WATCHINC

and sez:
"Eat Your Vegetal

leading trend in Anglo
American philosophy,
spurred by G. E.
Moore, John Austin,
and the oracular
Ludwig Wittgenstein.
A related trend was ex-
emplified by Gilbert
Ryle's influential *The
Concept of Mind,* 1949
which denied that con-
sciousness even exists.

Party behaviorism is anti-sexual as well as anti-mental. Body and mind alike are to be repressed . . .

The point of this is to narrow the likelihood of dangerous intimacy among the oppressed. With sexual love prohibited, libidinal energy is freed for war hysteria and hatred of Party enemies.

Party enemies include internal foes (the fabulous "Brotherhood" of Emmanuel Goldstein) and rival regimes. In all there are three global superpowers, each the mirror-image of the other:

Eurasia, ruled by the Neo-Bolshevik Party; Eastasia, ruled by the Death-Worship Party; and Oceania, ruled by the Ingsoc Party of Big Brother and O'Brien. (Oceania is made up mainly of North America and "Airstrip One," formerly England; "Ingsoc" stands for "English Socialism.")

Each superpower is supposedly the deadly enemy of the other two, but in reality "they prop one another up like three sheaves of corn." Permanent, limited war allows each ruling Party to maintain limited war hysteria indefinitely. (Internal opposition is less likely when external dangers seem great.) Never-ending war preparations also permit each Party to keep the proles in drudgery by maintaining artificial poverty.

All surplus is siphoned into military spending. The proles, as a consequence, are "stupefied" by economic hardship.

The Party tries hard to seem really invincible and permanent. However, in the *Newspeak* ''Appendix'' Orwell indicates that this appearance is unjustified—*Newspeak*, the appendix says, was the bizarre product of a failed dictatorship, which gave rise to a better society afterwards. But *claiming* immortality is central to the Party's purpose.

As Oceania's unique and unchallenged power, the Party is both Church and State. With Big Brother as its primary icon, the Party tries to fill the void created by the suppression of organized religion . . .

The special irony of the Big Brother personality cult is that Big Brother is entirely imaginary. The original Ingsoc revolutionaries have long since perished, mostly in the great purges of the sixties. Since then, Big Brother has been made the Party's symbolic representative.

Winston: ''Does Big Brother exist?'' *O'Brien:* ''Of course he exists. The Party exists. Big Brother is the embodiment of the Party.'' *Winston:* ''Will Big Brother ever die?'' *O'Brien:* ''Of course not. How could he die?''

For a confirmed atheist like Orwell, this makes Big Brother a mythical icon on a par with the Holy Trinity.

The Party is real, however, and it aspires to God-like omnipotence. Wrathful and vengeful in Old Testament manner, the Party's whim is law. It claims immortality: ''The rule of the Party is forever.''

Also immortal is the great enemy of the Party, Emmanuel Goldstein, leader of the shadowy revolutionary Brotherhood— Lucifer to Big Brother's God. A pioneer Ingsoc revolutionary, Goldstein now survives, apparently, only as a hated symbol. He serves as a lightning rod for public resentment—"an object of hostility more constant than either Eurasia or Eastasia."

The *Animal Farm* precedent for this—"when anything went wrong it became usual to attribute it to Snowball"—derived, originally, from Orwell's reflection on Trotsky's murder: "How will the Russian state get on without Trotsky? Probably they will be forced to invent a substitute."

Party rituals are patently religious. The daily Two-Minute Hate, focusing hostility on Goldstein's democratic plea, finishes with the sheep-like chant, "B-B! . . . B-B!"

O'Brien: "Reality exists only in the mind of the Party, which is collective and immortal." Winston, coming up for air, finds this even "more terrifying than mere torture and death. The Party could thrust its hand into the past and say of this or that event, *it never happened.*"

Correcting the past is precisely Winston's job at the Ministry of Truth. With a word into the *speakwrite*, Winston converts a fallen bureaucrat into an *unperson*. Every trace of that person vanishes; all books and papers are changed or burned.

Rectifying the past is something Winston enjoys and
does well, despite his aversion to the idea. What
Winston does less well, however, is practice *doublethink*. "Medically, I believe, this manner of thinking is
called schizophrenia; at any rate, it is the power of
holding simultaneously two beliefs which cancel out."

Every Stalinist shifting with prevailing Russian winds shows
a trace of this: "The unquestionable dogma of Monday
becomes the damnable heresy of Tuesday, and so on." Not
that Orwell acquits capitalism: "When one looks at the
all-prevailing schizophrenia of democratic societies, the lies
that have to be told for vote-catching purposes, the silence
about major issues, the distortions of the press, it is tempting
to believe that in totalitarian countries there is less humbug."

> *Doublethink* is the capacity to believe that Poland is
> a "People's Democracy," that South Africa
> belongs to "the Free World," that war manu-
> facturers comprise "defense industry."

O'Brien, in the torture chamber, tells Winston that to be
sane he must believe that $2 + 2 = 5$. (In the thirties the
Soviet Union urged a "Five-Year Plan in Four Years";
posters went up proclaiming that "$5 = 4$" and
"$2 + 2 = 5$.") Winston resists *doublethink,* then tries to
embrace it. But "reality control" eludes him. Only after
long psychic torture does he finally think doubly.

1984 begins with Winston vaguely upset. Born in 1944, the same year as Orwell's son, Winston is weary of drab London life (dingy Victorian buildings, rubble, no privacy, an occasional bombing from the Eurasian war; *i.e.*, the London of 1941). More importantly, Winston seethes with rage. Scolded by exercise leaders (who watch him through the telescreen) and observed by the Thought Police, Winston is repressed and self-repressing. His sexual frustration turns to fury.

6079 SMITH! BEND LOWER....!

Before Julia introduces herself, Winston sees her from afar—and hates her. "Vivid, beautiful hallucinations flashed through his mind. He would tie her naked to a stake and shoot her full of arrows like Saint Sebastian."

In the Two-Minute Hate, which had been designed to beam "a hideous ecstasy of fear and vindictiveness" on Goldstein, Winston finds his rage free-floating— attaching now to Julia, now to Big Brother. When he starts an illicit journal, Winston finds himself helplessly, compulsively writing "Down with Big Brother" over and over.

Julia, a seeming star of the Junior Anti-Sex League, is a 26-year-old mechanic assigned to a novel writing machine. After she daringly begins an affair with Winston, she explains "that sexual privation induces hysteria, which is desirable because it transforms into war fever and leader worship."

Sexual love heals Winston. He stops drinking, stops coughing, gains weight; his ulcer subsides. "The process of life had ceased to be intolerable. He no longer had any impulse to make faces at the telescreen or shout curses at the top of his voice."

Knowing that their romance will bring retribution from the Party, Winston and Julia decide to oppose the Party frontally. They approach O'Brien, hoping to gain entry into Goldstein's Brotherhood—in the mistaken belief that O'Brien is a friend and a revolutionary.

Prior to their arrest, Julia and Winston expect to survive spiritually no matter what happens. *Winston:* "If they could make me stop loving you, that would be the real betrayal." *Julia:* "That's the one thing they can't do. The can't get inside you."

In the words of the concentration camp song, "*die Gedanken sind frei*" (thoughts are free).

O'Brien thinks differently: "When finally you surrender to us, it will be of your own free will." Shattering torture in the Ministry of Love proves him right. In a glowing all-white environment, black-shirted Thought Police beat Winston senseless. Then O'Brien's interrogation, the fear of rats, and electro-shock leave him spiritless.

Emptied, Winston is refilled with love of Big Brother. Julia is also broken. When they later meet by chance, nothing happens. The spark is extinguished . . .

The most puzzling aspect of *1984* is Orwell's treatment of the proles. At times, they seem to be forgotten altogether. O'Brien, for example, says at one
point that it is "intolerable to us that an erroneous
thought should exist anywhere in the world." Then,
just a few pages later, he dismisses the idea that
proles need regulation.

"They are helpless, like the animals. Humanity is the Party.
The others are outside and
irrelevant."

The proles simply do
not seem to count in
1984, except as
props.

Even the most dim-
witted Outer Party
member—*e.g.*,
Parsons, "an unques-
tioning, devoted
drudge of paralyzing
stupidity"—is
shown to nurse sub-
conscious feelings of
rebelliousness (bab-
bling "Down with
Big Brother!" in his
sleep). Proles are
supposedly less
dangerous.

Even Emmanuel Goldstein's revolutionary book says that workers are "too much crushed by drudgery" to be revolutionary or troublesome: "From the proletarians nothing is to be feared. They can be granted intellectual liberty because they have no intellect."

Roughly 275 million proles make up 85 percent of the population of Oceania. (There are six million Inner Party members and 40 million Outer Party members.) In the vast equatorial "disputed territories" there are hundreds of millions of "slaves." All, apparently, are equally inert.

THIS PICTURE IS CLEARLY ABSURD. IT BEARS ASKING WHY ORWELL DREW IT.

Orwell was amazed at public lethargy during the war.

"In the face of terrifying dangers and golden political opportunities, people just keep on keeping on, in a sort of twilight sleep in which they are conscious of nothing except the daily round of work, family life, darts at the pub, exercising the dog, mowing the lawn, bringing home the supper beer, etc."

Even the prospect of an all-destroying nuclear war "is widely accepted with a sort of vague resignation. Everyone is intent on having a good time."

This echoes a comment made, much earlier, about the hanging of a Burmese thief. What seemed most pathetic to Orwell, as an observer, was that the thief *carefully stepped around a puddle*—as if it mattered, a minute away from death.

In a negative mood, Orwell might easily have felt that "having a good time" in the shadow of nuclear war is equally pathetic. Caricaturing the big public as "eternally" passive might have been Orwell's way of remonstrating with people over their fatal present passivity.

In any event, Orwell clearly knew that the real-life proletariat is not invertebrate. His continuing hope for a Socialist Europe rested on the expectation that European workers could be mobilized for socialism in the not-too-distant future. Why, then, did Orwell present such a one-sided picture?

It could be argued that, implicitly, Orwell *did* present a more dimensional picture. Julia, for example, though ostensibly an Outer Party member, is clearly a metaphor for the proles: warm-hearted, a handworker, sensual, non-intellectual, irreverent, bent on having a good time. Julia is bored by politics, both revolutionary and official. *Yet Julia rebels.*

It would be only slightly fanciful to see Winston and Julia as a metaphor for Orwell's fondest hope, the alliance of workers and the middle-class. But if this is so, Orwell does not make his meaning vivid. He draws the proles as cartoon characters, without showing that beneath the surface there lies repressed depth.

Orwell's sharpest statement is a paradox: "Until they become conscious the proles will never rebel, and until after they have rebelled they cannot become conscious."

In his essay on Koestler, Orwell had stated a solution to this paradox: "A 'change of heart' must happen, but it is not really happening unless at each step it issues in action."

Impelled to small acts of rebellion, workers register small gains in consciousness, which then permit further action; and so on. This seldom happens smoothly, but the essential process is clear.

Neither the saint, says Orwell, purely concerned with spirit, nor the revolutionary, purely concerned with outward change, is adequate. The best qualities of each must be synthesized.

Unfortunately, *1984* leaves this perspective unstated.

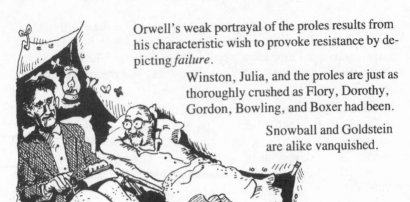

Orwell's weak portrayal of the proles results from his characteristic wish to provoke resistance by depicting *failure*.

Winston, Julia, and the proles are just as thoroughly crushed as Flory, Dorothy, Gordon, Bowling, and Boxer had been.

Snowball and Goldstein are alike vanquished.

You'll wanna read this one. It shows why we gotta drop the Bomb on the Bolshies!

The problem with this unrelieved portrayal of defeat is that it can reinforce passivity rather than undermining it. The response to *Animal Farm* gave Orwell every reason to understand this. Yet *1984* reproduces this mistake. Neither the Brotherhood nor the workers are given the ghost of a chance. *1984* is, for this reason, a ''flawed masterpiece,'' says biographer Bernard Crick.

The great Marxist historian Isaac Deutscher, who briefly shared war correspondent quarters with Orwell in Germany, tells of encountering a news vendor in New York who forced a copy of *1984* into his hands as the book Deutscher ''must'' read to learn why evil Russia should be destroyed. (Deutscher had just finished the definitive biography of Stalin.)

''Poor Orwell, could he ever imagine that his own book would become so prominent an item in the propaganda of Hate Week?''

Orwell did, in fact, have a taste of the anti-Communist interpretation to be conferred on *1984,* and he strenuously protested. He wa
embarrassed, he said, by "some very shame-making publicity"
emanating from "U.S. Republican newspapers." From his hospi-
tal bed in 1949 Orwell dictated a disclaimer to his publisher, Fred
Warburg, which stands as a kind of testament.

Conservative critics have
proven unfazed by Orwell's direct statement of his views—the
January 1984 *Reader's Digest,*
for example, simply dismisses
it—but anyone genuinely interested in Orwell will find this
compelling.

"It has been suggested by some reviewers of
1984 that it is the author's view that this, or
something like this, will happen inside the next
forty years in the Western world. This is not
correct. I think that, allowing that the book is
after all a parody, something like *1984 could*
happen. This is the direction in which the world
is going at the present time.

"Specifically the danger lies in the structure imposed on
Socialist and on Liberal capitalist communities by the
need to prepare for total war with the U.S.S.R. and by
the new weapons, of which of course the atomic bomb is
the most powerful. But danger lies also in the acceptance
of a totalitarian outlook by intellectuals of all colors.

"THE MORAL TO BE DRAWN FROM THIS DANGEROUS
NIGHTMARE SITUATION IS A SIMPLE ONE :
DON'T LET IT HAPPEN. IT DEPENDS ON YOU."

''George Orwell assumes that if *1984*-type societies come into being, there would be several super states, either opposed to each other or (a novel point) pretending to be more opposed than they really are. Two of the principal superstates will obviously be Anglo-America and Eurasia. The Anglo-Americans will plainly not take the name of their opponents *i.e.,* 'Communists.' Thus they will have to find a name for themselves. *1984* suggests 'Ingsoc,' but a wide range of choices is open. In the U.S.A. the phrase 'Americanism' or '100 percent Americanism' is suitable and the qualifying adjective is as totalitarian as anyone could wish.''

Shortly after dictating this statement, Orwell's powerful voice was stilled forever. His ideas, however, continue to resonate with conviction—and urgency. For a world bedeviled by war, oligarchy, nationalism, and the profit-motive, Orwell's prescription—socialist democracy—remains as vital and valid as ever.

Planet Orwell

Citizen 2 + Citizen 2

When, in early 2013, the 28-year-old
intelligence analyst Edward Snowden
reached out to journalists to say that
he had documentary proof that the
NATIONAL SECURITY ADMINISTRATION
was illegally amassing a vast trove of
data on private US citizens—whether
or not they were suspected terrorists—
he called himself "Citizenfour."

This pseudonym, and Snowden's
cautious use of encrypted messaging,
reflected the habits he had acquired while
working, since 2006, for the CIA in Geneva,
at the CIA's headquarters in Langley, Virginia,
and as an outside contractor for the CIA and NSA.

It also reflected a distinctly Orwell-like sensibility.

On May 20, 2013, Snowden flew to Hong Kong, where, after
staying quietly in a hotel room to await their arrival, he met with
the documentary filmmaker Laura Poitras and the journalist and
constitutional attorney Glenn Greenwald. He gave them a vast
cache of leaked classified files—at least 50,000—showing the
breadth of the NSA's domestic spying. He also authorized them to
reveal his identity.

Snowden's revelations first appeared in print on June 5, 2013.
Soon after, he was charged with espionage. Denied asylum in
many countries, he soon found himself alone in a hotel room,
again—in Moscow, where he had been granted temporary asylum.
Top United States officials called for his execution. *Citizenfour had
become, and remains, a fugitive.*

Snowden accepted this risk to make his point. *"Know,"* he told
Poitras, *"that every border you cross, every purchase you make,
every call you dial, every cellphone tower you pass, friend you
keep, [and] site you visit...is in the hands of a system whose
reach is unlimited, but whose safeguards are not."*

Edward Snowden has often been compared to Winston Smith.

He's slight, bookish, and he served the real-world Ministry of Truth. Arundhati Roy, who met Snowden in Moscow with Daniel Ellsberg and John Cusack, found him to be "much smaller than I thought he'd be. Small, lithe, neat, like a housecat." *Quiet and mild—like Winston Smith.* And he, too, speaks up for individual liberties.

"Do we want to live in a controlled society or do we want to live in a free society? That's the fundamental question we're being faced with."

Speaking in July 2014, Snowden added:

"*Nineteen Eighty-Four* is an important book but we should not bind ourselves to the limits of the author's imagination. Time has shown that the world is much more unpredictable and dangerous than that."

In 2013 Snowden said that Big Brother's technologies, "microphones and video cameras, TVs that watch us, are nothing compared to what we have available today. We have sensors in our pockets that track us everywhere we go. Think about what this means."

The uproar caused by Snowden's leaks put the government on the spot. President Obama offered this defense of the NSA's spying:

"*In the abstract, you can complain about Big Brother and how this is a potential program run amok, but when you actually look at the details, then I think we've struck the right balance.*"

THE DETAILS, WHICH WE OWE TO EDWARD SNOWDEN, ARE TRULY EYE-OPENING.

Wags have called the National Security Agency the only arm of government that actually listens to the public. Snowden showed the kernel of truth in that joke. The NSA obtained records from the phone companies about every call they handled, domestically and internationally. In all, three levels of surveillance were revealed:

"*Upstream programs*," which intercepted internet data in transit; *data mining programs*, which accessed Facebook, Google, Microsoft, YouTube, and other services to gather and store e-mails, chatroom posts, internet phone calls, login IDs, photos, videos, and more; and *spyware*, which used special software to create fake pages that run invisible malware on private computers.

These revelations sparked protests and unmasked NSA doublespeak. Under oath before the Senate in 2013, just months before Snowden's leaks came to light, Director of National Intelligence **JAMES CLAPPER** was asked for "a yes or no answer to the question, *Does the NSA collect any type of data at all on millions or hundreds of millions of Americans?*"

Clapper's response was firm: "No, sir."

Senator Ron Wyden: "It does not?"

Clapper: "Not wittingly."

When Snowden's leaks disproved this testimony, Clapper offered a creative defense: *"I responded in what I thought was the most truthful, or least untruthful manner, by saying no."*

General **KEITH ALEXANDER,** who had directed the NSA since 2005, stepped down amid swirling controversy. An appeals court ruled the mass surveillance illegal, and the program was terminated in 2014.

Not everyone was pleased . . .

Least untruthful?

Stepping Down?

You losers!

That wasn't the end of the story. In June 2014, Congress passed the "USA Freedom Act," which allows the NSA to gather much of the same data from sources outside the US. As the Pulitzer Prize–winning journalist Charlie Savage explains, given "the way the Internet operates, domestic data is often found on fiber optic cables abroad."

And since the surveillance laws do not apply in this case, the "Freedom Act" actually permits data collection with even less supervision than ever.

Welcome to Planet Orwell, *where the web is "world wide"—and we're all ensnared.*

Outside the United States, during the early years of the Iraq War, the CIA began to abduct alleged terror suspects—*seized without charges, by fuzzy criteria*—to be tortured at secret "black sites." On December 31, 2011, Obama signed into law the National Defense Authorization Act (NDAA) of 2012, which legalizes what the American Civil Liberties Union characterizes as "indefinite military detention without charge or trial...for the first time in American history."

"The NDAA's dangerous detention provisions would authorize [Obama] —**and all future presidents**—to order the military to...indefinitely imprison people captured anywhere in the world, far from any battlefield. . . .

"No one should live in fear of this or any future president misusing the NDAA's detention authority. The... provisions must be repealed."

The **Two-Minute Hate** could become a **Ten-Year Sentence**...

On June 25, 2016, Russia's parliament authorized prison terms for internet dissent. A charge of "extremism" could result in eight years behind bars. Encouraging "mass disturbances" could earn a ten-year sentence. And phone and internet providers, including Facebook and Telegram, would be required to store all messages for months or years to help the Russian intelligence agencies decipher encrypted messages.

The next day, Edward Snowden tweeted that this **"Big Brother law"** is an "unworkable, unjustifiable violation of rights" that **would take "liberty from every Russian** without improving safety."

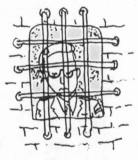

On July 7, when President Vladimir Putin signed this bill into law, Snowden tweeted: "Putin has signed a repressive new law that violates not only human rights, but common sense. **Dark day for #Russia."**

Putin, of course, has a long and brazen history of high crimes and human rights violations.

On his very first day in office— January 1, 2000—Putin flew behind the Chechen front to dramatize his support for the scorched-earth war against Chechen secessionists.

As television cameras rolled, Putin gave elite soldiers hunting knives engraved with his name.

Putin's critics seldom fare well. On October 7, 2006, the journalist Anna Politkovskaya was shot to death in Moscow. She had regularly chronicled abuses in the anti-Chechen war and she was an implacable foe of autocratic rule.

"We are hurtling back..." she wrote in 2004, "into an information vacuum that spells death from our own ignorance."

"All we have left is the internet, where information is still freely available."

"For the rest, if you want to [work] as a journalist, it's total servility to Putin. Otherwise, it can be death, the bullet, poison, or trial."

Six weeks after Politkovskaya's murder, another Putin critic, the former intelligence agent Alexander Litvinenko, died in London after becoming the first person known to have been poisoned with polonium-210.

In 2016, the British government concluded that Putin was "probably" guilty of ordering this radioactive murder.

"Order is the guarantee of freedom."

Edward Snowden has also criticized China's new Cybersecurity Law (2016), which Human Rights Watch calls "abusive." The law requires internet firms to censor "forbidden" materials that "damage national unity" or convey "false" news. In 2015, President Xi Jinping insisted at an internet conference that "order is the guarantee of freedom."

Maintaining online order, courtesy of the "Great Firewall," has long been a government priority. Dissident posts about the Tiananmen massacre, ethnic disputes, and strikes are routinely stricken from the web.

Xi Jinping has concentrated power in his hands to a rare extent (more than any Chinese leader since Mao Zedong) by assuming personal control over the economy and the military. All party members have been ordered to study Xi's "important thoughts" and many have signed pledges of absolute loyalty.

And apparently—as if that were enough— Xi aspires to a cult of personality.

Who is Xi Dada?

In 2012, a fan club began to call him Xi Dada, which means, roughly, "Big Daddy Xi." In 2015, on the eve of his visit to the United States, the *People's Daily* released a video, *Who Is Xi Dada?,* which showed young exchange students rhapsodizing about the president. One said he bought Xi's book and "would actually love to read it." Two others called him a "little bit cute" and "super charismatic." After Xi starred in a military parade, a virally popular song advised women to "marry someone like Xi Dada" who is "decisive" and will never stop fighting the "flies," "tigers," "monsters," and "freaks" of corruption.

Mass purges of rivals followed, accompanied by relentless efforts to restrict privacy and independence.

In 2015, the government reported that it would build a nationwide system in which "social credit scores" would be assigned to every citizen. In late 2016, it was announced that a pilot social credit project was underway in many locales, in preparation for national implementation by 2020.

The system's intent is conveyed by its inimitable slogan:

"Allow the trustworthy to roam everywhere under heaven while making it hard for the discredited to take a single step."

Data for the new credit system will come from personnel files, court records, loan and tax files, social media posts, internet histories, and files assembled by neighborhood committees like the Yanjing Sincerity Construction Office, which divides people into "red" (trustworthy) and "gray" (untrustworthy) groups. Penalties will be levied for "scores" of violations, including jaywalking, overdue bills, and traffic infractions. High scorers will have fast-track access to jobs, education, travel, health care, and even pets.

All this, says activist Zan Aizong, is "just like *Nineteen Eighty-Four*." The Western press agrees: "Big Data meets Big Brother." Or even, we might say: *Big Data meets Xi Dada*.

But by now, of course, even big brother plays the orwell card...

KOSACHEV

When **MICHAEL FLYNN**, Donald Trump's new National Security Advisor, resigned in early 2017 after it emerged that he had illegally assured Russian officials that sanctions for meddling in the 2016 election would be lifted, Konstantin Kosachev, the chair of the Foreign Affairs Committee in Russia's upper house of parliament, waxed indignant. Flynn was persecuted, Kosachev complained, for "thought crime (in the words of the immortal G. Orwell)."

Everyone, it seems, now wants to claim Orwell for themselves.

The Orwell Wars

When the first section of this book appeared in 1984 under the title **Orwell for Beginners,** Orwell's satires were famous but Orwell himself was much less well known.

Serious readers had been able to consult a four-volume collection of his essays, journalism, and letters (edited by Sonia Orwell and Ian Angus) since 1968, but the first major biography, by Bernard Crick, did not appear until 1980.

And even as late as 1979, several editors of the *New Left Review* were still able to predict, with fashionably "orthodox Marxist" confidence, that *Nineteen Eighty-Four* would be "a curio in 1984"— not unlike the glass paperweight that Winston Smith found in Mr. Charrington's shop in the prole district.

Orwell on the beach in Morocco

At this juncture Orwell the man, like the wider arc of his life and work, was still fairly obscure.

His critics could still hope that his memory might fall into oblivion.

That prospect sank like a stone in 1984. The *anno Orwellium* witnessed a flood tide of publications, including *Orwell for Beginners*, and the tide has never turned.

Since 1984, the swelling interest in George Orwell has yielded a bounty of new discoveries, some of which complicate our understanding of the man and his works. We now know that Eric Blair first attracted police attention in Paris in 1929, before he became "George Orwell"; that the CIA funded an *Animal Farm* film, which they gave a Cold War spin; and that Orwell, late in life, gave a British government agency a secret list of writers and speakers he regarded as politically unreliable.

The latter discovery, in particular, has raised questions about Orwell's commitments. Critics and defenders have taken strong stands—often hastily. My goal is to enhance the discussion with insights from the 10 thick volumes of essays and letters that appear in *The Complete Works of George Orwell* (1998 and 2006, edited by Peter Davison et al.) along with a newly discovered manifesto that Orwell wrote with Bertrand Russell and Arthur Koestler in defense of peace and democracy.

> ***What do we learn from these neglected documents?*** That in Planet Orwell, we are asked to choose between oligarchical collectivism and authoritarian capitalism. But Orwell fought for something entirely different—*a planet of libertarian socialism*.

On December 4, 1948, the very day on which he sent the finished manuscript of *Nineteen Eighty-Four* to his publisher, Orwell also wrote to his friend, the contrarian critic Malcolm Muggeridge. In that letter, which came to light only recently, Orwell disagreed with Muggeridge on a point of principle, arguing:

"Authoritarianism," in 1948, would soon become a world-famous concept. *The Authoritarian Personality*, by Else Frenkel-Brunswik, Theodor W. Adorno, R. Nevitt Sanford, and Daniel Levinson, appeared in 1950, just two months after Orwell's death—and is now recognized as perhaps the most influential work of 20th-century social psychology.

Originally inspired by Erich Fromm's study of German workers on the eve of Hitler's ascent to power, *The Authoritarian Personality* found a connection, which has often been found since, between the "sadistic" wish for a harsh, domineering ruler to punish the weak and despised and a "masochistic" wish to surrender personal autonomy and liberty. "Soft" leaders are anathema to people with authoritarian tendencies; only wrathful rulers, who rule imperiously and harshly, are admired.

Orwell had hoped for insights of this kind, writing, in 1944, that the connection "between sadism, masochism, success-worship, power-worship, nationalism, and totalitarianism is a huge subject whose edges have barely been scratched, and even to mention it is considered somewhat indelicate."

"To take merely the first example that comes to mind, I believe no one has ever pointed out the sadistic and masochistic element in Bernard Shaw's work, still less suggested that this probably has some connexion with Shaw's admiration for dictators."

SHAW

As it happens, as Stephen Ingle notes, G. K. Chesterton had already criticized Shaw's "incredibly caddish doctrine that the strength of the strong is admirable but not the valour of the weak." But Orwell's point was effectively made nonetheless.

Intellectuals who admire dictators, he added, resemble "the efficiency experts who preached 'punch,' 'drive'... and 'learn to be a Tiger man' in the 1920s" and that "older generation of intellectuals, Carlyle...and the rest of them, who bowed down before German militarism."

"It is important to notice," Orwell went on, "that **the cult of power tends to be mixed up with a love of cruelty and wickedness *for their own sakes.* A tyrant is all the more admired if he happens to be a bloodstained crook as well."

When Orwell wrote these lines, Fromm's survey was unpublished and the surveys that yielded *The Authoritarian Personality* had just begun. But Orwell's intuitions were confirmed when these studies appeared. So too was his sense that many people would recoil from the "indelicate" implications of this way of thinking.

Bob Altemeyer, who is today's leading student of authoritarianism, has called the wish for punitive authority "mean-spirited." Yet many people regard even that term as indelicate—despite the fact that high scores on authoritarianism scales reflect a willingness to "stomp out" dissent; discriminate against women, immigrants, and minorities; undermine democracy; and tolerate, or even take satisfaction in, the misery of "the undeserving poor"—including children.

Resisting authoritarianism, in this sense, was Orwell's highest value. His libertarianism, meanwhile, was not the cult of deregulated markets that has become the debased latter-day meaning of that term. Rather, as a chorus of his friends attests, Orwell's libertarianism was *socialist*.

JULIAN SYMONS:

Orwell "remained a libertarian Socialist until he died, and those who read into *Nineteen Eighty-Four* a change in his essential beliefs are mistaken."

FENNER BROCKWAY agreed.

He recalled that, after *Animal Farm* was published in August 1945, Orwell "was

emphatic
that he remained
a libertarian socialist."

What this meant to Orwell in practice, Brockway added, was support for industrial and local democracy. George Woodcock amplified this point, saying that Orwell favored a "decentralized society and workers' control of industry... with a great deal of room for individual initiative."

In 1941, when Orwell thought the war might end in revolution, he proposed radical reforms including nationalizations (of big industries, banks, etc.), income ceilings, and "classless" schools. In 1945, when the Labour Party won the first postwar general election and Clement Attlee became prime minister, Orwell said that even a moderate socialist government should aim for similar reforms:

ATTLEE

"A Labour government may be said to mean business if it (a) nationalizes land, coal mines, railways, public utilities and banks, (b) offers India immediate Dominion status (this is a minimum), and (c) purges the bureaucracy ... to forestall sabotage from the Right."

Significantly, Orwell wrote this just days after *Animal Farm* appeared—and it was *Animal Farm* that created the impression that Orwell had renounced socialism. That impression, he soon explained, was seriously mistaken...

Joy Batchelor and John Halas were the British filmmakers who were secretly funded by the CIA to make the feature-length animated film version of Animal Farm *(1954).*

Dwight Macdonald, who edited the journal *politics*, was another of Orwell's confidantes in the 1940s. An anti-Stalinist iconoclast—a war resister and a libertarian socialist—Macdonald wrote to Orwell in late 1946 to say that some of his associates interpreted *Animal Farm* as a warning that revolutions always misfire, "hence to hell with it and hail the status quo." That, Macdonald said, *"doesn't seem correct to me."*

The sclerosis of the revolution is often dated to 1921, when the Bolsheviks crushed a democratic sailors' revolt at Kronstadt.

Right, Orwell replied—that isn't correct: "I meant *that kind* of revolution (violent conspiratorial revolution, led by unconsciously power-hungry people) can only lead to a change of masters."

"I meant the moral to be that revolutions only effect a radical improvement when the masses are alert and know how to chuck out their leaders as soon as the latter have done their job. The turning point of the story was supposed to be when the pigs kept the milk and apples for themselves (Kronstadt)."

"If the other animals had had the sense to put their foot down then, it would have been all right."

n short, Orwell told Macdonald: "What I was trying to say was,

You can't have a revolution unless you make it for yourself; there is no such thing as a benevolent dictatorship.'"

This conclusion is also Orwell's reply to mandarin critics of *Animal Farm* like his friend, the poet T. S. Eliot, who had written to him to say his "pigs are far more intelligent than the other animals, and therefore [they are] the best qualified to run the farm— in fact, there couldn't have been an *Animal Farm* without them: so that what was needed (someone might argue) was not more communism but more public-spirited pigs.

ELIOT

When Pigs Fly?

For Orwell, expecting freedom or true reform from public-spirited pigs, or oligarchs of any kind, is folly.

Like every ruling stratum, the self-serving pigs of *Animal Farm* batten on the fruits of underclass labor, in this case, *apples*.

o sharpen this point, to reply in advance to objections like liot's, Orwell added new lines to the radio version of *Animal arm* in 1948:

CLOVER: "Do you think it is quite fair to appropriate the apples?"
MOLLY: "What, keep the apples for themselves?"
MURIEL: "Aren't we to have any?"
COW: "I thought they were to be shared equally."

Equality, Orwell held, can be won only by resistance...

The Utopian Orwell

By now the public is so familiar with the iconic image of **ORWELL THE PROPHET OF DYSTOPIA**, that many people would be surprised to learn that, on the eve of writing *Nineteen Eighty-Four*, Orwell called himself an unrepentant utopian. The context was a series of 1946 articles in which he offered a typology of the "many serious thinkers" who
"are dissatisfied with both *laissez-faire* capitalism and the Russian form of Socialism."

Here, as was often the case, Orwell's attention orbited around the intelligentsia. Though he was a faithful advocate of workers control, he was ultimately more interested in the literati than he was in labor per se. This became obvious in *Nineteen Eighty-Four,* in his wafer-thin, stereotypical portrayal of the somnolent heedless proles. But it was true long before then as well.

Orwell's writings are full of reflections on themes of immediate practical concern. But rare indeed is even a stray, passing remark on industry, the trade unions, or the day-to-day realities of the Labour Party.

When Orwell reflects on authoritarianism, he has intellectuals in mind. Stalinism, for his purposes, is more an ideology than a social system.

At heart, Orwell is a representative, and critic, of the writing class—a class he regards as fatefully divided.

Orwell and his BBC colleagues, including T. S. Eliot, during World War II

Besides distinguishing authoritarians from anti-authoritarians, Orwell also distinguishes between *types* of anti-authoritarianism. In all, he posits four distinct trends: *pessimism, utopianism, pacifism,* and *Christian reformism.* All are "in revolt" against unfettered capitalism and Russian-style oligarchical collectivism. But otherwise they differ greatly.

Under the heading **Christian Reformers,** Orwell lists his friend Eliot and Eliot's predecessors Chesterton and Hilaire Belloc, whose "Distributism" envisaged a return to small private farming and worker-owned cooperatives.

BELLOC

Under the heading **Pacifism,** with a tendency "towards Anarchism," Orwell lists Herbert Read and Aldous Huxley.

CHESTERTON

He gives them credit for rejecting statism, but otherwise he offers pungent criticism, arguing that pacifists can be tempted to appease fascist aggression.

Of far greater concern to Orwell than Distributism and pacifism, however, was the essential distinction he drew between pessimism and utopianism.

Pessimists, *"tending towards Conservatism,"* *'deny that a planned society can lead either to happiness or to true progress."*

Utopians, *whom Orwell also calls left-wing socialists, favor democratic planning with a high level of individual liberty.*

Influential pessimists *include Friedrich Hayek, Peter Drucker, James Burnham, F. A. Voigt, and Orwell's close friend Malcolm Muggeridge.*

Utopian luminaries *include Victor Serge, Franz Borkenau, Freda Utley, Ignazio Silone, John Dos Passos, and Orwell's close friend Arthur Koestler.*

The issue here is utopia, *Yes or No*.

Pessimists, Orwell says, are essentially anti-utopians. "The term 'pessimist' fits all of these writers in so much as they refuse to believe in the possibility of an earthly utopia." This refusal is grounded in an underlying misanthropy, the conviction that "human wickedness" is "original" and incorrigible. If human nature is depraved, campaigns to perfect society will also be depraved. Generations of anti-utopian punditry were prefigured by Voigt's extrapolation from this premise—his claim, in *Unto Caesar* (1938), that movements "to establish the 'earthly paradise' always end in tyranny":

"His basic argument is quite simple. A statesman who aims at perfection... will stop at nothing. ...Perfection, in practice, is never attained, and the terrorism used in pursuit of it simply breeds the need for fresh terrorism."

Voigt's pessimism was rooted in the conviction that Stalinism and Nazism, which were nearing their apogee, were "perfectionist" utopian creeds.

Stalin's executioner, Yagoda, who was ultimately executed himself

Similar arguments came from Hayek, Drucker, and Muggeridge for whom perfectionism and totalitarianism were near synonyms. Burnham, meanwhile, was an extreme case, denying that political decency is even *possible*. On that basis, he urged a morality that Orwell regarded as impossible—public-spirited *Machiavellianism*.

Utopians, for Orwell, are neither pessimists nor Machiavellians. Despite an occasional "superficial resemblance," "there is no real affinity between dissident Socialists like Koestler...and enlightened Conservatives like Voigt. "The point is that a Socialist...believes the 'earthly paradise' to be possible. *Socialism is...an optimistic creed and not easy to square with the doctrine of original sin."*

But neither are they perfectionists. Few socialists believe "that human society can actually be made perfect, but almost any Socialist *does* believe that it could be a great deal better...and that most of the evil that men do results from the warping effects of injustice."

Utopians want planning and industry, but they do not believe that this requires the sacrifice of liberty. They adhere to "the older conception of Socialism," which affirmed "equality [and] human brotherhood."

The "genealogy" of these ideas—"the ideas for which writers like Koestler and Silone stand"—include Marx and Anatole France; "Utopian dreamers" like William Morris and "mystical dreamers" like Walt Whitman;" Gerrard Winstanley, "the Digger from Wigan"; early Christians, and rebel slaves.

WINSTANLEY, 1649: *"ENGLAND IS NOT A FREE PEOPLE, TILL THE POOR THAT HAVE NO LAND HAVE A FREE ALLOWANCE TO DIG AND LABOUR IN THE COMMONS."*

It would not be unreasonable to think, Orwell stressed, that today's "Utopians, at present a scattered minority, are the true upholders of Socialist tradition." Since 1917, however, the word "Socialism" had become profoundly ambiguous. Stalin's *"SOCIALISM IN ONE COUNTRY"* and Hitler's *"NATIONAL SOCIALISM"* had muddied the waters.

This raised a fundamental question:

"Can you have Socialism without liberty, without equality, and without internationalism? Are we still aiming at universal human brotherhood, or must we be satisfied with a new kind of caste society in which we surrender our individual rights in return for economic security?"

KOESTLER   SILONE   SERGE   UTLEY   BORKENAU

Orwell found "perhaps the best discussion" of these questions in Koestler's book *The Yogi and the Commissar* (1945). For Koestler, "revolutions have to happen, there can be no moral progress without drastic...changes," and yet revolutionaries who forfeit "ordinary human decency" are morally lost. Politically, "this means rejection of Russian Communism on the one hand and of Fabian gradualism on the other."

Gradualism, of the kind espoused by the Fabian Society, had always been so hesitant as to border on paralysis; and, quite peculiarly, some of the leading Fabians, in the 1930s, had opted for what Orwell could only regard as the worst of both worlds, snail-like gradualism in Britain and whole-hearted support for Stalin's Russia. Sidney and Beatrice Webb were leading representatives of this trend...

THE WEBBS

Orwell's criticism of Soviet Russia pivoted largely around his opposition to Stalin's purges and persecutions, which he had seen at first hand in Spain and which harmed millions of ordinary Russians. But Orwell was also critical of what he regarded as Lenin's subversion of socialist principle. In a neglected book review written while he was writing *Nineteen Eighty-Four*, he traced Stalin's terror, in part, to the inner nature of Bolshevism:

"Originally, 'Communism' meant a free and just society based on the principle of *'to each according to his needs.'*...Marx had envisaged an overwhelmingly powerful proletariat sweeping aside a small [capitalist class] and then governing democratically....*What actually happened was the seizure of power by a small body of classless professional revolutionaries, who claimed to represent the common people.*"

Ultimately, the vaunted Bolshevik
"DICTATORSHIP OF THE PROLETARIAT"
was little more than domination by
"A HANDFUL OF INTELLECTUALS"—
the writing class **over** the
working class.

THE DILEMMA THIS POSED FOR EGALITARIAN SOCIALISTS WAS TWOFOLD.

On the one hand, many members of the Western intelligentsia felt an affinity for the ruling intelligentsia in Russia. Even Stalin's monstrous crimes were extolled or excused. His apologists argued that idealistic "ends" justify brutal "means." Fascinated by Stalin's force and guile, his disciples were caught in the toils of an ethic that blamed victims and absolved the perpetrators of "necessary" murders.

Orwell was incensed when Stalinists excused the wartime murders of Victor Alter and Henryk Ehrlich, leaders of the Jewish Socialist Bund in Poland. His final verdict on the pro-Soviet Communist parties was nuanced but severe:

"In spite of much courage and devotion, the main effect of Communism in Western Europe has been to undermine the belief in democracy and tinge the whole Socialist movement with Machiavellianism."

A second dilemma was public indifference. "At this moment it is difficult for Utopianism to take shape in a definite political movement. The masses everywhere want security much more than they want equality [and they seldom] realise that freedom of speech and of the Press are of urgent importance to themselves."

Orwell was thus keenly aware of the obstacles facing egalitarian and freedom-loving socialism. But he did not relinquish his optimism. Even after Stalin's terror, Hitler's genocide, and World War II, Orwell did not give up hope that utopianism could still inspire a definite and practical political movement.

Orwell's Manifesto

At the start of 1946, just weeks before he wrote his articles on pessimism and utopianism, Orwell joined forces with his fellow utopian Arthur Koestler to found a new organization that would defend democratic rights, work to minimize the risk of a Cold War, and campaign for a lasting peace based on what they called **"psychological disarmament."**

This initiative has gone largely unnoticed, partly because it was short-lived— but also because the manifesto that Orwell drafted for this initiative (with Koestler and Bertrand Russell) vanished from sight—until recently.

That manifesto has now been found, and it appears here for the first time.

In writing this manifesto, by partnering with Koestler and Russell, Orwell was making an attempt to put his utopianism into practice. In his letter to Macdonald later in 1946, he rejected fatalism:

"If people think I am defending the status quo that is, I think, because they have grown pessimistic and assume that there is no alternative except dictatorship or laissez-faire capitalism.

Orwell did not share that premise. He was not starry-eyed about the future, but neither was he hopeless.

He saw the menacing prospects of the postwar era—above all, the danger that the world would divide into permanently warring oligarchies.

Peace and democracy, like equality and liberty, would vanish in such a world.

But Orwell refused to concede defeat—and he put that refusal into practice by taking what was, for him, a unique step—an attempt to organize directly, on an international scale, to define and defend democracy.

Orwell's partner in this utopian crime was Arthur Koestler.

Christmas in Wales...and a Plan to Save the World

The setting was idyllic. Orwell and his infant son, Richard, joined Arthur Koestler, Mamaine Paget (Koestler's fiancée), and Mamaine's identical twin, Celia, for Christmas in 1945 at the country home Mamaine and Arthur shared in Wales.

George and Richard befriended Celia, whom they met on the train to Wales; Richard was much livelier and noisier than his hosts had anticipated (he "howled," Koestler told a friend), but the holiday was a success...

The foursome got along famously...

CELIA PAGET

The Paget twins, whom Koestler later recalled
as "the brilliant Paget twins—stars, or rather
twin stars, among the debutantes of the 1930s"—
became fond of Orwell, and they were impressed
by his sure-footed parenting. (They ultimately
came to call him "Donkey George," after the
character Benjamin in *Animal Farm*.)

Years earlier, when Arthur first met George, he found him
remote and intimidating—"a real Burma sergeant." But they
warmed up to each other greatly. When, not long after the
holiday, George proposed to Celia, Koestler could hardly contain
himself. "Arthur practically went on his knees and implored me
to marry George," Celia recalled later, "because he simply loved
George, and he would have loved to have George as a brother-
in-law. He thought that was a wonderful idea."

Celia answered George in "rather ambiguous" terms. He got the
hint, but said "he'd like to go on being friends...so we went
on seeing each other." Before long, they were both active in a
campaign that George and Arthur had dreamed up in Wales.
The idea was to build a human rights group of a new kind—not
simply to defend political and social liberties, but to extend
them. And they hoped to achieve this on both sides of the
geopolitical divide that Winston Churchill, two months later,
would call the "Iron Curtain."

A Meeting of Minds...

Ten years earlier, Orwell and Koestler would not have been
allies. Both went to Spain in 1936 to fight fascism, but Koestler
served Stalin's Comintern and Orwell fought fascism *and*
Stalinism...

KOESTLER WENT TO **SPAIN** THREE TIMES IN **1936** AND **1937.**

HE WAS SENT BY WILLI MUNZENBERG, THE MASTERMIND OF THE COMINTERN'S AMBITIOUS EFFORT TO SPONSOR PRO-SOVIET FRONT GROUPS AND PUBLICITY ORGANS ACROSS EUROPE.

KOESTLER'S MISSION WAS TO WORK UNDERCOVER AS A FOREIGN CORRESPONDENT IN FASCIST TERRITORY, WHERE HE ATTEMPTED, WITH SOME SUCCESS, TO GATHER EVIDENCE PROVING THAT FRANCO WAS GETTING MILITARY HELP FROM HITLER AND MUSSOLINI, IN CONTRAVENTION OF INTERNATIONAL AGREEMENTS!

IN EARLY 1937, WHILE **ORWELL** WAS FIGHTING WITH A POUM MILITIA, KOESTLER WAS ARRESTED BY FASCIST POLICE AND SPENT SEVERAL HARROWING MONTHS IN **FRANCO'S PRISONS.**

THOUGH HE BROKE WITH STALINISM SHORTLY AFTERWARDS, KOESTLER'S MEMOIR, **SPANISH TESTAMENT (1937),** WAS INTENDED AS

COMINTERN PROPAGANDA!

ORWELL, WHO WROTE ABOUT KOESTLER IN 1944, WHEN THEY STILL KNEW EACH OTHER ONLY SLIGHTLY, WAS CHARITABLE ENOUGH TO SAY THAT, THOUGH PARTS OF THE BOOK WERE DISFIGURED BY SECTARIAN INTENT (SOME SECTIONS EVEN APPEARED TO HAVE BEEN "DOCTORED"), THE BOOK STILL HAD

REMARKABLE PASSAGES!

Darkness at Noon (1941) marked Koestler's definitive break with Stalinism. It was also his first attempt to explore what Orwell called his main theme, the atrophy of revolutionary imagination, as revealed by Stalin's terror. But Orwell suspected that Koestler's anti-Stalinism might ultimately devolve into anti-utopianism...

Writing in 1944, Orwell detected in Koestler's work a tendency toward the same "pessimistic Conservatism" of which he was to acquit him in 1946.

"Revolutions always go wrong—that is [his] main theme."

Orwell wrote that, over time, Koestler had come ever closer to the view that, in fact, "revolutions are of their nature bad....It is not just that 'power corrupts': so also do the ways of attaining power."

"Of course, Koestler does not say this explicitly, and perhaps is not altogether conscious of it"; but Stalin's crimes in Russia and Spain had sapped his optimism. His dwindling utopianism now took the form of the "quasi-mystical belief that for the present there is no remedy, all political action is useless, but that somewhere in space and time human life will cease to be the miserable brutish thing it is now."

Given this fatalistic premise, Orwell wrote, Koestler's best remaining choice is to be a "short-term pessimist, i.e., to keep out of politics, [to] make a sort of oasis within which you and your friends can remain sane"; hence, Orwell concluded, it was not surprising to detect a "well-marked hedonistic strain" in Koestler's writing —the hedonism of the political cynic for whom utopianism can now have meaning only *pianissimo*, personal life

Orwell the Organizer?

As we have seen, Orwell found reassurance in Koestler's next book, *The Yogi and the Commissar*.

It appeared that Koestler had regained his political optimism, to a modest degree at least.

And Orwell was further reassured by their visit in Wales.

It now seemed apparent that Orwell and Koestler held very similar views, not least on the unfolding dangers of the postwar world. They agreed that the fall of fascism was likely to bring the wartime honeymoon between capitalism and Stalinism to an abrupt end. And since both victorious systems were ruled by oligarchies—not identically, or to the same degree, but similarly—democracy would have to be defended in both realms.

Orwell had found a kindred spirit.

It seemed that Koestler was no longer a potential "pessimistic Conservative" but was, rather, a utopian, in Orwell's down-to-earth sense—a partisan of peace, in a world of unending war.

Their decision to collaborate, in Wales, was a kind of epiphany.

"I have never seen [Orwell] so enthusiastic," Koestler later reminisced, "as when we discussed the projected League." Among the names they considered for their new group was "Renaissance—A League for the Defence and Development of Democracy."

Their goal, they agreed, would be to lobby "against repressive laws" and for political prisoners "everywhere," from the US to the USSR. They hoped to publish a magazine, using the office of the new journal *Polemic*, for which Orwell was a board member and Celia Paget was an editorial associate. Their concept was to build an umbrella group that PEN and other groups could join *en bloc*. Koestler contacted Amis de la Liberté and Giustizia e Libertà and Orwell reached out, through the United Auto Workers, to an "American organisation...with which we should obviously be affiliated"—the International Rescue and Relief Committee, which numbered, among its national board members, the philosopher John Dewey and the novelists John Dos Passos and Upton Sinclair.

Back in Britain, Orwell and Koestler were particularly eager to enlist the philosopher Bertrand Russell, who, with his wife Patricia ("Peter"), lived near Koestler in Wales and would soon win the Nobel Prize for Literature (in 1950).

Orwell later told Dwight Macdonald that Russell had been one of the first to grasp Bolshevism (he cited Russell's memoir of a sojourn in Russia in 1920) and he and Koestler felt that Russell's worldwide fame would confer instant credibility on the new League.

Hence, when Orwell returned to London to write the first draft of the League's manifesto—which he sent to Koestler on January 2, 1946—Koestler's task was to broach the idea of the League to Russell. That tête-à-tête went well and Russell proposed holding a small conference, in Wales over Easter, to bring together key potential collaborators.

The challenge, Russell wrote, "is to persuade the human race to acquiesce in its own survival."

Orwell shared the plan with Dwight Macdonald and Mamaine told Edmund Wilson. Others they told included Freddie Ayer of *Polemic*, Jennie Lee, and Manès Sperber. Koestler asked Sperber to approach André Malraux, and Orwell met with Ignazio Silone.

Koestler applauded Orwell's draft, but Russell was critical. The full story of the ensuing dialogue with Russell (which lasted months and involved Mamaine Paget and Peter Russell) is a saga unto itself, often bordering on soap opera. Early bonhomie was followed by a stormy clash, which in turn was followed by a détente that made the quartet "palsie-walsies" again (as Mamaine told her "darling Twinney," Celia).

Privately, Koestler found Russell to be "impish, waspish, and donnish." Meanwhile, the Russells (especially Peter) found Koestler to be brusquely "Communist" in manner. But in the end, despite their conflicts, they patched over their political differences. When the clamor subsided, the manifesto had been modestly revised, and it was signed by both Koestler and Russell.

This is among the very few documents that Orwell ever coauthored, or wrote for organizational purposes. The aim was to deepen the concept of democracy, and to mitigate national antagonisms, at a time when peace and freedom were in doubt once again.

The window of opportunity for this initiative was open only briefly—the interval, lasting barely a year, from the end of World War II to the start of the Cold War.

If anyone finds it pretentious to call this text a "Manifesto," they are welcome to call it, say, a "Mini-festo."

Orwell wouldn't mind...

The Manifesto

" . . . without liberty
there can be no security."

*Drafted by **George Orwell** on January 2, 1946; revised in dialogue
with **Arthur Koestler** and **Bertrand Russell** through May 1946*

During the past fifty years it has become apparent
that the Nineteenth Century conception of liberty
and democracy was insufficient. Without equality
of opportunity and a reasonable degree of equality
of income, democratic rights have little value. But
the tendency, especially since the Russian revolution,
has been to over-emphasise this fact and to talk as
though the economic aspect were the only one, while
habeas corpus, freedom of speech and of the press,
the right to political opposition and absence of
political terrorism were merely phrases designed to
side-track the attention of the poor from economic
inequality. Both Communists and Fascists have
reiterated that liberty without social security is
valueless, and it has been forgotten that
without liberty there can be no security.

It is unquestionable that even in the western
countries—and perhaps especially in those
countries which have had no direct experience
of totalitarianism—there has grown up a certain
contempt for democratic traditions and a habit
of sanctioning tyrannous practices abroad or at
home, which would have raised an outcry a few
years ago. In this country the majority of people
are largely uninterested in and even unaware
of their democratic rights, while a considerable
section of the intelligentsia has set itself almost
consciously to break down the desire for liberty
and to hold totalitarian methods up to admiration.
Over considerable portions of the earth not merely
democracy but the last traces of legality in our
sense of the word have simply vanished.

But instead of this fact awakening the traditional indignation of the western peoples, the normal reaction is either apathy or a certain admiration for what it has become usual to call political realism.

As a result, we see liberal newspapers making themselves the advocate of totalitarian diplomacy and bodies such as the League for the Rights of Man and the National Council for Civil Liberties, which were started to defend the individual against the arbitrary action of the state, ending up by pursuing objects which are almost the exact opposite of those for which they were originally founded.

Since Nazism collapsed, the one great power with a totalitarian structure is the U.S.S.R., and it is chiefly in the form of uncritical admiration for the U.S.S.R. that totalitarian ideas establish themselves in the western countries. Meanwhile, the gradual decay of democratic sentiment, of human decency and the desire for liberty goes on, and if ultimately some autocratic regime were to establish itself in this country, in France or in the United States, or if those countries were to become the victims of aggression, the resistance to it would be much weaker because of the work that had been done beforehand by the theoretical apologists of the totalitarian type of "realism."

It is therefore felt that the time has come to form a new organisation to do the work which such bodies as the League for the Rights of Man were supposed to do and failed to do.

This League should have the two-fold task of (a) theoretical clarification and (b) practical action.

(A) A firm theoretical platform of clearly defined principles is essential to prevent the League from either degenerating into a vague gesture of goodwill or from being captured by any political party, caucus or other body of people likely to pervert its aims.

The first task of clarification is to re-define the term "Democracy" which is being interpreted in diametrically opposed ways in East and West, and thus loses all concrete meaning.

This re-definition is the more necessary as a repetition of 19th Century liberal principles is not enough. The programme of the Rights of Man has to be restated in the light of the experience since the French Revolution. In particular a synthesis has to be found between political freedom on the one hand and economic planning and control on the other. The starting point of the discussion should be to regard as the main functions of the State:

1. To guarantee the newborn citizen his equality of chance.

2. To protect him against economic exploitation by individuals or groups.

3. To protect him against the fettering or misappropriation of his creative faculties and achievements.

4. To fulfill these tasks with maximum efficiency and minimum of interference.

This task of clarification should be carried out by exchange of ideas in the League's quarterly and later monthly magazine, between individuals and group in various countries pursuing similar aims.

Such groups exist at present in various countries, particularly in the U.S.A., Mexico, Italy and France, but with little or no mutual contact. The international co-ordination of the activities of these groups both for theoretical and practical work should be the main aim of the League.

(B) The practical work of the League should be carried out by the methods employed by the old League of the Rights of Man, Committees of Vigilance, Civil Liberties, etc., on a broader and more intensive scale, by public meetings and direct influencing of members of the Press, Politicians, Authors and Scientists.

The League has to make itself the advocate of [resistance to] infringements against the Rights and Dignity of Men, whether they occur in the British Empire or in Russian occupied territory. It will fight for the defence of the individual against arbitrary arrest, imprisonment without trial, punishment under retrospective laws, arbitrary displacement or restriction of movement or of the right to nominate and vote for candidates of his own choice.

The committee of Founders and the Central Body of the League should consist of men of standing and integrity who cannot be regarded as servants of any sectional interest. The League should be open to men and women of all parties, races and creeds who subscribe to the principles outlined above and closed to all those who, for whatever ideological motives, condone infringements of these principles if carried out in the name of "higher interests" and thus become the instruments of totalitarian methods. It should be tolerant of divergent opinion but uncompromising in its fight against any tendency to subordinate ethical values to opportunistic expediency.

We have initiated this action driven by the sense of urgency in the age of the atomic bomb, by the realisation that individuals and groups in all countries are groping to find an expression for their aims, and by consciousness of the necessity to co-ordinate their energies.

We are sending you this rough draft to hear your reactions and suggestions. There is only one type of reaction that we are not anxious to hear: the answer that it is too late, that the evil has gone too far and can no longer be stopped by the methods visualised here.

"Too late" is the motto of escape into destruction.

This document, which is unique in many ways, could easily be misread. Readers might think that Orwell and his coauthors were ordinary civil libertarians, or Cold Warriors. But this manifesto is far from ordinary, and Orwell's intent was not to promote the Cold War but to avert it.

Equality from birth, freedom from exploitation, unfettered creativity

Orwell and his coauthors wanted a human rights group that, unlike established groups would resist the "decline in democratic sentiment.

In place of a narrowly legal notion of civil liberties they offered a wider concept of *democratic rights*

Since they agreed that liberty without freedom from poverty is incomplete, they sought democracy that would be economic as well as political socialist as well as liberal

It was rare, then as now, to demand equality for every "newborn citizen." Surveys show that "equal opportunity" is an ever-popular slogan. But when confronted with the implication of that slogan—that opportunities are only equal if they are equal from birth—many people hesitate, or refuse, to support policies to *assure* equal opportunities. Help for infants generally entails help, of some kind, to their parents as well; and many people would prefer to see children born into destitution than risk helping their "undeserving" parents.

By affirming equality as they did—quite literally, as a birthright—Orwell and his coauthors gave the concept of democratic rights a singularly humanitarian foundation. So too, by defending freedom from exploitation and the right to uncensored creativity, they sought to ground their appeal in core ethical principles that humanitarians of all kinds could support. It was in that spirit that Orwell and Koestler reached out to wary pessimists (Russell, Michael Polanyi) as well as socialists (Silone, Lee). Pessimism was acceptable as long as it did not lead to defeatism—to what the manifesto called "escape into destruction."

In short, Orwell and Koestler sought to unite socialism with liberalism, which, in this instance, took the form of civil libertarianism. And they hoped to oppose Soviet pseudo-socialism while seeking, at the same time, to reduce the animus between the Soviet Union and the West.

These, plainly, were ambitious goals. Were they contradictory?

The Case for Psychological Disarmament

The few writers who have noticed Orwell's association with Koestler generally assume that their collaboration was simply naïve. Others, however, charge them with cynicism. They say that, by repudiating grimly "realistic" excuses for Stalin's assaults on democracy, Orwell and Koestler were objectively taking sides in the Cold War—i.e., that they were cynically choosing one great power over another. The truth is more nuanced. Orwell did not simply assume that he could severely criticize Russia without succumbing to the Cold War.

Rather, he hoped that, on questions like this, the new League would pursue what the manifesto called "(a) theoretical clarification and (b) practical action." But in fact, tensions over Soviet Russia were present from the start, and they ultimately became acute, dividing Orwell from Koestler and Russell and putting the credibility of their ideas in doubt.

In early 1946 that tension was subliminal. But warning signs were visible in the difficult dialogue with the Russells over "psychological disarmament." Surviving excerpts from early drafts of the manifesto show that Orwell and Koestler wanted to propose measures to disarm the Soviet Union and the West "psychologically" as well as militarily. They warned that East-West tension had increased alarmingly in the six months since the end of the war, and that, if the wartime alliance frayed altogether, decades of conflict between rival oligarchies could ensue. But a solution was still possible: psychological disarmament. This would require, above all, free access to news and ideas of every kind, across every border.

Koestler called this the "crux" of what he and Orwell were advocating. They sought to make this notion concrete by proposing the following:

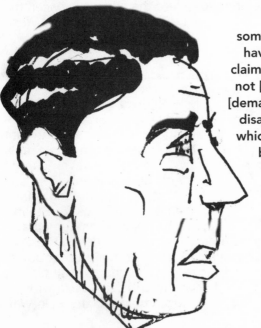

Since the end of the war some of the victorious nations have raised certain territorial claims. Great Britain, which has not [made such] claims, should [demand] general psychological disarmament, the first step of which would be an agreement between Great Britain and the USSR, based on the following points

(a) Free access to British newspapers, periodicals, books and films to the general public in the USSR and territories occupied and controlled by her and vice versa

(b) Such modifications of existing censorship regulations as to permit the free circulation of information about the outside world throughout both countries and territories occupied and controlled by them;

(c) The conclusion of an agreement between the Reuters and Tass Agencies [that each shall] compile a news summary of 500–1000 words per day which the other Agency undertakes to distribute for internal consumption. The news summary should be confined to a factual presentation of items relating to developments in internal politics, economy, the arts and sports, and its publication should be encouraged in the newspapers of both Government Parties and in the national Press.

The Russells objected that trading territory for policy was unwise, since territory, once acquired, can be held indefinitely, while policies can be changed at any time.

When the Russells insisted, further, that all references to psychological disarmament should be deleted from the text, Koestler was unhappy. This was, he recalled later, the manifesto's signature theme, "which had come to assume a central position in the draft after Orwell and I had rewritten it three or four times."

But when the Russells stood fast, Orwell and Koestler acceded to their wishes—and Koestler argued the case for psychological disarmament in the *New York Times* in March 1946.

In language adapted, it seems, from an early draft of the manifesto, Koestler renounced the wartime taboo that Western governments had imposed on criticism of Stalin's Russia. It was a mistake, he argued, to turn a blind eye to Soviet mistrust and hostility:

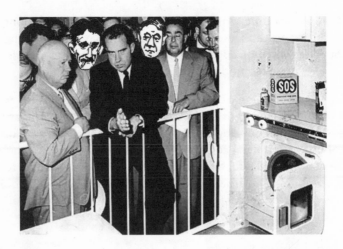

"World peace can only become a reality if suspicion is abolished. Suspicion can only be abolished if the Soviet Government can be induced to turn the master-switch of their propaganda factory. How can the Soviet leaders be induced to do this?"

"The first necessity is that our own statesmen should realise that no political treaties and trade agreements can guarantee peace as long as the world remains psychologically divided into two worlds, with persecution-mania on one side and growing alarm on the other."

Koestler asserted that not just military disarmament but *"psychological armaments should be made an object of international negotiations....* By 'psychological armaments' I do *not* mean criticism directed by one country against another. This democratic right is as vital on the international as on the national scale. . . ."

Rather, *"the measure of 'psychological armament' is the extent to which a government obstructs the free exchange of information and ideas with the outside world.* A country which builds a Maginot line of censorship from behind which it fires its propaganda salvoes is committing psychological aggression."

"Since the end of the war, the U.S.S.R. has raised certain claims in South-Eastern Europe, the Middle and Far East and North Africa. The Western Powers, who have no territorial counter-claims to make, should [put forward] instead a demand for *psychological disarmament*, including:

(a) free access to foreign newspapers, periodicals, books, and films to the U.S.S.R.;

(b) such modification of the Russian censorship (if censorship there must be) as to permit the free circulation of information about the outside world throughout Soviet territory;

(c) free access for accredited journalists, parliamentary committees, etc., to Russian-occupied territory;

(d) the abolishing of restrictions on travel for foreigners to Soviet territory, and for Soviet citizens abroad;

(e) active co-operation with the Western Powers in the organisation of 'vacations abroad' schemes, on a mutual exchange basis, for students, teachers, writers, workers and professional men."

Koestler added that, since Western Europe was a shambles in the wake of the war, exposure to the West would not excite the envy of destitute Russians, as it would have earlier.

Hence, Stalin had little to fear from cultural exchange, 'if the iron curtain is lifted."

The war of ideas would take the place of armed warfare—and while the result might be antagonistic, it would be a conflict of minds, not arms.

Koestler's conclusion was daring: "Psychological disarmament would almost automatically lead to material disarmament...and the present vicious circle would be reversed." To clarify this extraordinary claim, he suggested several steps to make cultural disarmament a reality:

Nobody in his senses will expect the Soviet leaders to agree to this easily. Hence...psychological disarmament should be made a bargaining object in future negotiations....If I were a politician, I would gladly swap the North Persian oil, plus a trusteeship in North Africa, for the acceptance of these demands.

The demand for the free circulation of ideas across frontiers, for restoring the arrested bloodstream of the world, should be raised at every meeting of the Big Three, the Security Council, the Committees and Assembly of the United Nations; it should be made the precondition of concessions in the geographical, economical, and scientific field.

To get it accepted, the use of all levers of pressure, political and economical, would for once be morally justified.

This is plainly more than a standard affirmation of democratic rights. It reflects the wish to *extend* democracy, not simply to defend it.

Could this scheme have worked?

We'll never know, because the window of possibility closed shortly after it opened.

Orwell's first draft of the manifesto was written seven months after the end of the war.

Another seven months later, in August 1946, Stalin's deputy Andrei Zhdanov violently criticized the West and rejected any prospect of free cultural exchange.

ZHDANOV

Soon after, the Cold War was in full swing. By fall Orwell had retreated to an island in the Hebrides, where he began *Nineteen Eighty-Four*. His manifesto was never widely circulated, and the concept of psychological disarmament went unnoticed. Recently, however, a number of critics have depicted this concept as a kind of literary Trojan Horse for anti-Soviet politics. For these critics, Orwell and Koestler figure more as Cold Warriors than as neutral avatars of a new vision of democracy.

Is this interpretation valid? It's true that Orwell, Koestler, and Russell saw Stalin's dictatorship and anti-Westernism as the single greatest obstacle to postwar peace. But were they anti-Soviet in the banal Cold War sense? Orwell always denied that charge. Understanding his views on this subject requires nuanced insight.

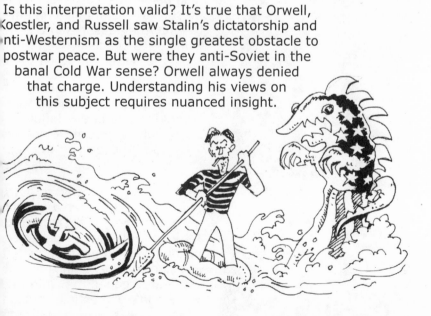

Stalin's Purges, from Barcelona to Moscow

Stalin's purges, as Eric and Eileen Blair experienced them in Spain, are the touchstone of Orwell's politics after 1936. His friendship with Koestler sprang from their horrified fascination with Stalin's purges, of which Koestler remains a central chronicler. Many of Orwell's essays discuss the purges, and *Nineteen Eighty-Four*, like *Darkness at Noon*, focuses on purge victims who confess under psychological duress.

In July 1937, Stalin's agents in Spain charged Eric and Eileen Blair with being *"trotzquistas pronunciados"* who served Hitler. That same month marked the start of the bloodiest phase of Stalin's purges, the "Great Terror." Had the Blairs not fled Spain just weeks earlier, they could easily have shared the fate of their comrade Bob Smillie, who died in a Spanish prison— officially, of appendicitis—in June 1937.

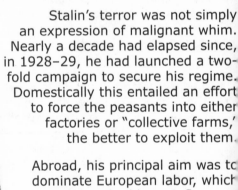

Stalin's terror was not simply an expression of malignant whim. Nearly a decade had elapsed since, in 1928–29, he had launched a two-fold campaign to secure his regime. Domestically this entailed an effort to force the peasants into either factories or "collective farms," the better to exploit them.

Abroad, his principal aim was to dominate European labor, which until then had been influenced mainly by Social Democrats. By 1937 these two campaigns were bordering on disaster.

In 1932, Hitler had come to power when Stalin's followers refused to vote with the Social Democrats. Although Hitler had won several million fewer votes than the left wing parties, they split their vote —and reaped the whirlwind. Stalin's domestic campaigns were also *in extremis*.

Rapid industrialization had always been a Bolshevik goal, but Stalin pursued that goal with impatience and breathtaking brutality. Once he had vanquished the relatively moderate Bukharin and Trotsky, he chose to work *against,* rather than *with,* the peasants, whose long communal history was well known—and now, overthrown.

In this way Stalin turned millions of farmers into wage-workers on state-owned "collective farms."

Millions of others, meanwhile, were flung to the four winds, becoming vagrants in a chaotic diaspora; still others were plunged into a rapidly swelling factory proletariat. All this happened against the backdrop of the Great Depression, and as the global economy stumbled from crisis to crisis, anarchy threatened. Stalin's policies, which telescoped into a few years what capitalism had taken an epoch to achieve—converting peasants into proletarians—had torn the social fabric. Shortages and famines were acute and wages were low. The result was discord and disorder, especially in ethnic minority regions like Chechnya, where several thousand insurgents took up arms in the early '30s.

Totalitarian repression was Stalin's survival strategy. A critical phase began in 1933 when Stalin declared "class war" on crime and disorder.

Attempts to flee famine-stricken areas were harshly punished and over two million displaced peasants were branded as bandits and "antisocial elements" and repressed by means just as extreme as those used against displaced farmers in 16th-century England, which Marx in *Capital* called "grotesquely terroristic."

"Clearing operations" drove "undesirables" to wintry wastes. Difficult ethnic minorities were deported. Workers were prodded and pushed. A campaign to intensify production, called "Stakhanovism," pressed workers to emulate the record-breaking coal miner Stakhanov.

One of Orwell's anarchist friends, Marie Louise Berneri, showed in a booklet how Stakhanovism, which Stakhanov modestly said should be called "Stalin's Movement," divided relatively better paid workers, who exceeded production quotas, from workers paid starvation wages.

Resistance to Stakhanovism was punished as sabotage. But soon, amid a brewing legitimacy crisis, the party sought to deflect the workers' anger from the inner party to managers and union officials, many of whom had favored Bukharin or Trotsky at some time.

STAKHANOV

BERNERI

The Show Trials

This was the setting in which the Moscow Show Trials took place from August '36 through March '38. Thanks to German rearmament and the Spanish war, the survival of the Soviet Union was in question, and Stalin's grip on power was far from secure.

It was at this point that Stalin turned his police loose on party leaders, many of whom had been his rivals in the past. The firs major victims were his former co-rulers Grigory Zinoviev and Lev Kamenev, who had helped him oust Trotsky after Lenin's death in 1924. They, like many other Old Bolsheviks, were seasoned organizers who still wielded personal influence. For an insecure dictator, they were a threat.

ZINOVIEV AND THE MOSCOW TRIAL

Trotsky, in exile, openly presented himself as Stalin's rival and rightful successor. Zinoviev and other Old Bolsheviks who remained in Russia were not equal threats—but they too could succeed a faltering tyrant. So Stalin undertook decisive action to eliminate that danger.

Isaac Deutscher, in his biography *Stalin* (1949), which Orwell read just months before his death in January 1950, said that an easing of terror still seemed possible in early 1936.

Even after Zinoviev and Kamenev had been jailed, hopes for their release did not seem in vain.

Bukharin still edited *Izvestia* and Radek pronounced on foreign policy. But instability was rife. The working class was riddled with discontent, as Deutscher observed: "Here and there workers assaulted...Stakhanovites and smashed machines." Stalin was worried by the strength of the anti-Stalinist left in Spain, which, as before in Germany, he labeled fascist.

KAMENEV

In August '36, Zinoviev and Kamenev were the main defendants in the "Trial of the Sixteen." Stalin's prosecutor, Vyshinsky, accused them of terrorism and collusion with Hitler. No defense attorneys were present. No witnesses were called. No evidence was given beyond "confessions."

Of the defendants' guilt Vyshinsky permitted no doubt. His summation was eloquent in its brutal complacency:

"Horrible and monstrous is the guilt of these criminals... who raised their hand... against Comrades Stalin, Voroshilov, Zhdanov."

"The fields of countless collective farms are rich with a golden harvest. Thousands of new...Stakhanov factories ... are pulsating with life."

"These mad dogs of capitalism tried to tear limb from limb the best of the best....To chain them is not enough."

Zinoviev and the others were, in fact, summarily executed. But their removal was not Stalin's only goal. What he wanted most was shown by Vyshinsky's wishful rhetoric, in which he imagined a "mighty wave of popular wrath, now sweeping from one end of the country to the other against these despicable murderers."

Stalin, no less wishfully, likened his party to Antaeus, the son of Gaia and Poseidon. Antaeus was so strong that he seemed invincible. But in fact he sprang up with new vigor each time he was knocked down because he gained energy from the earth his mother

The proletariat, said Stalin is our Gaia

Attempting to realize this fantasy the party pressed workers across Russia to denounce the traitors But few responded

ubashov, the imprisoned oppositionist in Koestler's *Darkness
t Noon*, asked his jailer, "Do you really think the people are
till behind you?" Answering his own question, he said *"No"*: "It
ears you, mute and resigned,...but there is no response in its
epths."

he Great Terror

n September 1936, Stalin replaced Yagoda, the terror chief,
ith the even more ruthless Yezhov. That same month Piatakov,
 senior industrial leader and ex-Trotskyist, was charged with
eason.

ays later, an explosion in Siberia killed 10 miners. This
ave Stalin the pretext for a trial of mine officials and former
ppositionists, the "Trial of the 17." This concluded in January
ith another round of executions. But this was all still prologue.

n the "Great Terror" from June 1937 through 1938, persecutions
f "hallucinatory" intensity (in Deutscher's words) became even
arsher.

irst came the secret trial and execution of top military officers.
ext came Yezhov's "mass operations," the intent of which,
e said, was to eradicate "once and for all" the menace posed
y vagrants, dissidents, ex-landowners, fractious ethnicities,
nd religious sectarians. The aim was to stem flight from
he collective farms and to stifle dissent among workers, the
nemployed, and the 1.5 million ex-party members who had
een expelled for being "alien or harmful elements."

ezhov's operations were truly massive. Over 2 million people
ere arrested, including 767,397 "Category 1 or 2 enemies."
our hundred thousand were deported or interned and another
67,000 were shot. There was some resistance—including
 renewed insurgency in Chechnya—but that, too, was
ercilessly suppressed.

Senior party members were decimated. By late 1938, two-thirds of the delegates to the 1934 Party Congress were in custody. In March 1938 Bukharin and 20 others were victimized in the final show trial.

Other purge victims included top Comintern leaders, a past premier, two vice premiers, and Polish, German, and other foreign communists who had sought refuge in the USSR. In some provinces nearly half of those caught in Yezhov's net were manual workers. In 1940, Yezhov himself became one of the Great Terror's last victims.

Fake History ... and the Real Winston Smith

By 1938 nearly every leader of the Bolshevik revolution of 1917 had been executed or denounced. So Stalin ordered a team led by Pyotr Pospelov, the former *Pravda* editor, to prepare a revised history of the revolution in which these leaders would appear as fascists and plotters. The result was Pospelov's *Short Course* on the history of the revolution.

This book, though false in every way, became what a classified US intelligence report called perhaps "the largest selling book in the world." When Stalin died in 1953, 41 million copies of the *Short Course* were in print in 67 languages.

It was the most successful example of the fake history that Orwell detested—a Ministry of True propaganda narrative of the kind that Winston Smith, imitating Pospelov, would write for Big Brother.

Unsurprisingly, the nimble Pospelov ultimately led the team that prepared Premier Nikita Krushchev's official 1956 exposé of Stalin and the staged Moscow trials.

POSPELOV, IN PERSON AND
ON A POSTAGE STAMP

For Pospelov, as for Stalin and Big Brother, history was elastic. It was written by the winners of the moment for the aims of the day. Orwell understood this early, and he fought back.

Echoes of the Terror

In a 1937 review that the *New Statesman* had invited but refused to print, Orwell called the Communist Party "an anti-revolutionary force."

"Fascism is being riveted on the Spanish workers under the pretext of resisting Fascism; ...since May a reign of terror has been proceeding and all the jails...are crammed with prisoners who...are half-starved, beaten and insulted."

Not long after fleeing Spain in 1937, Orwell was disgusted to learn that his friend Stafford Cottman—who, at 17, had been the Independent Labour Party's youngest volunteer in Spain and had served under Orwell's command—was the target of a hate campaign by the Young Communist League (YCL).

Orwell attended a rally to defend Cottman, who was denounced by the YCL with a verdict as clichéd as it was sectarian:

> "We brand him as an enemy of the working class."

Cottman's home, Orwell told a friend, was being "shadowed" by YCL members "who attempt to question everyone who comes in."

"What a show!" Orwell exclaimed. "To think that we started off as heroic defenders of democracy and only six months later [we] were 'Trotsky-Fascists' sneaking over the border with the police on our heels."

STAFFORD COTTMAN

But Orwell, of course, was undeterred. In the years after his return from Spain, he embarked on an odyssey with many twists and turns. Anti-Stalinist to the core, he nonetheless embraced the USSR-UK-US alliance against Hitler. Later, he fought to preserve this alliance and the amity he hoped it would spark...

The World Turned Upside Down

When, on August 23, 1939, Stalin signed a pact with Nazi Germany, the USSR's priorities shifted decisively. Since Hitler was now an ally, Stalin pivoted away from his earlier anti-Nazism, redefining Germany as a Russian ally and turning a baleful eye on Western and especially British imperialism. On September 1, 1939, when Britain and France responded to Hitler's invasion of Poland by declaring war on Germany,

British communists were told to embrace "REVOLUTIONARY DEFEATISM"— that is, to make Britain's defeat their highest priority.

The CPGB, Britain's Communist Party, quickly fell into line. Until the invasion of Russia by Germany in June 1941, the party fought hard to stir anti-government feeling among workers, soldiers, and the general public. This dismayed many sympathizers, including Victor Gollancz, John Strachey, and Harold Laski of the Left Book Club. Gollancz, who broke from the party most sharply, was inspired by Orwell's book of essays, *Inside the Whale* (1940), of which he was also the publisher.

In the title essay, Orwell offered a diamond-sharp critique of Stalin's about-face.

"While I have been writing this essay another European war has broken out.... Almost certainly we are moving into an age of totalitarian dictatorships."

STRACHEY   GOLLANCZ   LASKI

Anticipating the concerns that he would later voice in his manifesto with Koestler, he added that World War II, while necessary, "will either... tear Western civilization to pieces, or... end inconclusively and prepare the way for yet another war which will do the job once and for all."

What worries me at the present," Orwell confided to Gollancz, is the uncertainty as to whether the ordinary people in countries like England grasp the difference between democracy and despotism well enough to want to defend their liberties." He was, more immediately, perturbed by the CPGB's capacity for arrant self-contradiction. "Every time Stalin swaps partners, 'Marxism' has to be hammered into a new shape. This entails sudden and violent changes of 'line,' purges, denunciations,... etc."

"Every Communist is... liable at any moment to have to alter his most fundamental convictions."

The good news was that orthodoxy was restricted to the "inner ring" of insiders, while "soft-boiled" sympathizers (he cited the Left Book Club) were vulnerable to cognitive dissonance.

That dissonance became visible in *The Betrayal of the Left: An Examination & Refutation of Communist Policy from October 1939 to January 1941*, edited by Gollancz with essays by Orwell, Strachey, and Laski.

The authors were not all on the same page. Strachey defended the Moscow trials and insisted, in Ingsoc-like fashion, that "the fact that the Soviet Union is totalitarian does not mean that it is not Socialist."

Orwell, of course, disagreed. He held that dictatorship over the state and the means of production is the precise opposite of socialism—that in fact, as he wrote in a review of Franz Borkenau's *Totalitarian Enemy* (1940), Soviet society is a form of "OLIGARCHICAL COLLECTIVISM."

Actual socialism is "revolutionary and democratic."

Orwell also now offered a global critique of Stalinism, making two arguments: that, in Spain, Germany, and elsewhere, Stalinism had fatally divided the working class, thereby opening the door to fascism; and that the Stalinist intelligentsia had displayed a fatal gift for deceit, which opened the door to political betrayal and intellectual dishonesty.

Both of these tendencies had come to the fore in 1929–1934, Orwell wrote, when Stalin advanced the line "that 'Social-fascism' (i.e., Socialism) was the real enemy of the workers and that capitalist Democracy was in no way whatever preferable to Fascism."

Under the leadership of Ernst Thälmann, German Communism took this sectarian line as gospel. The result was that the working class was divided in two, and when Hitler took advantage of this division to take power, "thousands of German Communists" fled to safe havens in the parliamentary West.

"By their action," Orwell said, "they had belied their words."

THÄLMANN

Nazi rule was savage, infinitely worse than Social Democracy in Germany in the 1920s, or parliamentary rule elsewhere.

Of Tables and Duck Ponds

ULBRICHT

One German Stalinist who fled, not to Paris or London, but to Moscow, was a prime object of criticism in *Betrayal of the Left* —Walter Ulbricht, who later ruled East Germany.

Ulbricht, whose name was mistakenly but phonetically spelled "Ulbright" in *Betrayal*, was one of the likely prototypes for the paradigmatic figure of O'Brien in *Nineteen Eighty-Four*.

He proved his talent for steely illogic in an article in 1940, in which he attacked the eminent socialist Rudolf Hilferding, who had called for democratic and socialist unity against Nazism.

Ulbricht professed to be shocked—shocked—that Hilferding would side with France and England against Nazism. The German workers, he huffed, "do not wish to exchange the present régime for a régime of national and social oppression by British imperialism and German big capitalists who [serve] Britain."

The German Communists, Ulbricht roared, call it "criminal madness" for Social Democratic leaders "to believe they can end this regime in Germany by means of a reactionary war.... [It is all] the more criminal because the force which, according to Hilferding, will decide the war's outcome, *is the world's most reactionary force*"—British imperialism.

Of course, Ulbricht insists, this does not imply solidarity with Hitler. But—but!—Stalin was right to condemn the Western press for stoking "hatred against Germany," since Germany "had declared itself ready to establish peaceful relations" with Russia.

This position was not original. In October 1939, *Izvestia* had echoed what Molotov said the day he signed the pact: "One may respect or hate Hitlerism.... This is a matter of taste. But to undertake war 'for annihilation of Hitlerism' means to commit criminal folly."

MÜNZENBERG, KOESTLER

Koestler, in the same period, had a memorable encounter with Ulbricht's colleague, Gerhart Eisler.

Koestler had been in Paris, editing a socialist journal for his mentor Willi Münzenberg, who had broken with Stalin.

But when the worried French interned suspect Germans Koestler and Eisler were both among them

Interned next to Eisler, Koestler asked whether he would refuse to assist the Allies against Hitler

Eisler said yes

In the ensuing argument, Koestler marveled that "everything [Eisler] said sounded utterly convincing."

"One could almost hear the well-oiled cogs turn in his brain and grind the words out of their meaning, turn them round and round until it became self-evident that real anti-Fascism meant support for the Fascists."

Koestler's reaction resembled that of the novelist **HEINRICH MANN**, who, in 1937, had written about Ulbricht:

"I simply can't sit down at the same table with a man who suddenly claims that the table at which we are sitting is not a table at all but a duck pond and expects me to agree with him."

On June 22, 1941, Hitler invaded Russia—and Stalinists were again fervent in their hatred for Hitler, and adamant that they had always been the truest anti-fascists. The duck pond was suddenly a table again.

EISLER

MANN

Writers of the World, Unite

Orwell found a glimmer of hope, as he wrote in 1941, in the birth of "the 'political book,' a sort of enlarged pamphlet combining history with political criticism." This genre, pioneered by "renegades" from extremism "who have seen totalitarianism" at close quarters ("Trotsky,...Silone, Borkneau, Koestler"), was a bracing departure from the anodyne clichés of prefascist literature, whether liberal or Marxist.

Writers in this new genre were uniquely alive to the power of **war fever, fanaticism, race-hatred, and leader-worship**— and they neither underestimated Hitler nor made excuses for Stalin. But they did not equate Nazism and Stalinism either. For Orwell, Nazism was incalculably worse than Stalinism—not a revolution betrayed, but counter-revolution incarnate.

When, thanks to Hitler's invasion, Russia changed sides, Orwell welcomed the new alliance. Hitler was now everyone's enemy #1. That made Hitler's defeat, and postwar peace, far more likely. When, in 1942, a formal treaty was signed, Orwell was over the moon: "It would be almost impossible to over-estimate the significance of this event." Until then, Russia and its allies had been "attacked by the same enemy" but were "liable to...new disagreements" after they defeated that enemy. Now, though, Russia and Britain, backed by America, had signed a 20-year pledge "to restore peace, order, and a decent standard of living."

In this burst of enthusiasm, we see the 1946 manifesto prefigured. But we also see the spirit of an earlier manifesto, which Orwell and Koestler had signed with Cyril Connolly and five others in late 1941.

"**Why Not War Writers? A Manifesto**," called upon the British government to support creative writers across the political spectrum. "It is no longer possible...to stand back and call the war an imperialist war. For every writer, the war is a war for survival." The manifesto added that political books, in the new sense, also had roles to play.

"A novel will create a picture which will not be effaced by to-morrow's newspaper.... During the Spanish War, writers...such as Hemingway, Malraux and Silone exerted a deeper influence than journalists."

MALRAUX

Cyril Connolly later called this manifesto the "most lost of lost causes." But Orwell soon proved its point. With *Animal Farm*, barely two years later, he emerged as one of the ablest of political novelists—warning, at the outset of the postwar years, that allied oligarchies (of pigs and farmers) could not be trusted to ensure civil rights without pressure from below. But the problem, as he and Koestler agreed later, was that the existing human rights groups were inadequate.

Purging the Truth. Orwell said the strangest thing about the Moscow trials was not "that they happened—for obviously such things are necessary in a totalitarian society—but the eagerness of intellectuals to justify them." It was distressing, in particular, to see civil liberties groups rush to defend the trials, as happened in both France and Britain. When he sent Koestler the draft manifesto, Orwell recalled that the French League for the Rights of Man in France "had [gone] Stalinist..., as I...remember that it refused to [help] Trotskyists in Spain." His memory was accurate.

Fifty years earlier, amid the tumult of the Dreyfus affair, militant liberals who opposed antisemitism founded the Ligue des Droits de l'Homme. But by 1936 the Ligue's liberalism had turned inside out. Raymond Rosenmark, a former counselor to the Soviet Embassy, was asked to review the purge trials. He admitted the absence of defense attorneys, witnesses, and evidence, but he insisted—and the Ligue's leaders agreed—that "to doubt the... confessions would [betray] ...scientific thought."

There were dissenters. One voiced disbelief that the Ligue would tolerate a miscarriage of justice "100 times" worse than the Dreyfus affair. But when Magdeleine Paz and 2,000 others called for an impartial commission to review the trials, the Ligue's leaders said *No*.

ÉMILE GUERRY said that he "platonically" regretted the death sentences, but that revolutions cannot afford moral purity; they must, accept "relative justice" and avoid even indirectly...attacking the leaders of the Soviet democracy."

"Even if their justice was summary, they are entitled to a good deal of understanding from the sons of the French revolution which was, at times...a bit quick to judge and somewhat heavy of hand."

This, plainly, was precisely the kind of cynical "realism" that Orwell and Koestler would later reject so sharply. Ultimately, when Paz and others left in protest, the Ligue was free of dissent. A similar "realism" appeared in Britain, where the National Council for Civil Liberties was the Ligue's equivalent. In 1934, the NCCL leader wrote to a leading Stalinist to say that the NCCL would "keep to the correct party line" and would give few opportunities "to the 'liberals' for deviation." He kept his word, and soon the NCCL's most distinguished Keeper of the Line was D. N. Pritt, King's Counsel and later MP, who served on the NCCL's executive committee from 1934 until 1960.

Described by the leader of the Socialist International as Vyshinsky's "famous advocate in Western Europe"—given his standing as "one of the ornaments of the British Bar"—PRITT was tireless in his defense of the trials, writing articles and the pamphlet *The Zinoviev Trial* (1936).

This did not go unnoticed in Moscow, where, at the Second Session of the Supreme Soviet, it was noted that "the English lawyer Pritt has several times stated in print that the Soviet courts are carrying out the most advanced ideas into practice."

Pritt was, in many ways, Orwell's exact opposite. After the Zinoviev trial in 1936 he wrote that Russia had taken "a very big step towards eradicating counter-revolutionary activities" and "establishing their reputation among the legal systems of the world." He knew that "faint-hearted socialists are beset with doubt" but ultimately, he said, "it will be realized that the charge was true, the confessions correct, and the prosecution fairly conducted."

Above all, Pritt rejected any hint that Stalin and Vyshinsky were the truly guilty parties: "If [we] dismiss...the prosecution as a 'frame-up,' it follows inescapably that Stalin and...other high officials [were] guilty of a foul conspiracy." Pritt dismissed that possibility, declining, like the French Ligue, "to blacken the rulers of a Socialist country."

Orwell was not wrong when, in 1944, he called Pritt "perhaps the most effective pro-Soviet publicist" in Britain. Walter Krivitsky, who had been a Soviet military intelligence chief, said that Pritt served as Vyshinsky's publicist. "His mission was to write up the trial in such a way that it would be accepted" in Europe. An intercepted Comintern cable to the CPGB ordered the printing of Pritt's pamphlet in many languages: "All our publishers are informed."

Later, in response to articles by Trotsky's son, **LEV SEDOV,** another Comintern cable issued this command: "Organize answer by Pritt."

Pritt later became the leading British defender of the Nazi-Soviet pact—and when Hitler invaded Russia, he reversed course and declared, with cheery aplomb, that Hitler's aggression proved that the CPGB, and only the CPGB, had been right all along.

Awarded the Stalin Prize in the 1950s, Pritt remained faithful, to the bitter end, to every one of the party lines he had ever upheld.

SEDOV

Walter Krivitsky, like Pritt's handlers, took writers seriously. Shortly after his break with Stalin, he publicly urged the Nobel Prize–winning novelist Romain Rolland to renounce the Moscow trials. Rolland had commemorated the 20th anniversary of the 1917 revolution with a salute to Stalin for reviving the "interrupted" work of the Jacobins: "...*the new world, which we dreamed, you built. Hail to Stalin the builder.*" Rolland ignored Krivitsky's plea.

ROLAND AND HIS IDOL

Doublethink, and a grim "realism," were on the march.

Of Haters and Mad Hatters

When Orwell and Koestler decided to compete with the NCCL, they were already extremely unpopular with Pritt and his friends. Pritt's occasional coauthor, Randall Swingler, and the party philosopher John Lewis, were among their earliest and fiercest critics. *Animal Farm* and *The Yogi and the Commissar* had struck nerves. But the Zhdanov-like tenor of the criticisms they received from Swingler, Lewis, and others did not deter them. Orwell and Koestler wanted Russia and the West to disarm psychologically *because* mutual hostility was still rife.

LEWIS, SWINGLER

Zhdanov's speech ultimately dashed that hope. But even before then, the unreliability of their own allies had begun to cast shadows over the disarmament project. The mercurial Russell was the first to spin out of orbit. A year earlier, in August 1945, he had published an article just days after the destruction of Hiroshima and Nagasaki in which he had listed several ways to avoid future wars, including, as a "less utopian" option, for the United States to use its momentary atomic monopoly "to insist upon disarmament, not only in Germany and Japan, but everywhere except in the United States"—*and to ensure the realization of that outcome by force*, or the threat of force.

That was a passing remark in an ephemeral article, but it was peculiar nonetheless. So was Russell's less-than-humanitarian conclusion: "I fear that respect for international justice will prevent Washington from adopting this policy." Another grim realism was rearing its head …

That realism reappeared, even more vividly, in a second Russell article that appeared in *Polemic* in the summer of 1946, just months after he signed the manifesto. He leaped further into the void, concluding his article with a line that had emerged from his dialogue with Orwell and Koestler—"the difficulty is to persuade the human race to acquiesce in its own survival"—but otherwise arguing very, very differently.

In the name of an icy realism, he broached the possibility of building a world state that would monopolize atomic power; or, alternatively, of forging an alliance led by the US and Britain, that would enlist the USSR "by a mixture of cajolery and threat, making it plain to the Soviet authorities that refusal will entail disaster."

If Russia acquiesced willingly, all would be well. If not, it would be necessary to bring pressure to bear, even to the extent of risking war, or in that case it is pretty certain that Russia would agree."

This was not quite an endorsement of preventive atomic war, but it was aggressive in the extreme. Orwell expressed his own views about atomic warfare in 1947 in an essay on a book in which James Burnham openly advocated preventive war by the US on the USSR. Orwell was implacable. Advocating unprovoked nuclear war is unconscionable, and Burnham's wish to outlaw Communist parties was little better.

BRITTAIN

Orwell did not invariably oppose harsh measures in wartime. During the war he argued against blanket criticisms of aerial bombing of German cities by Vera Brittain and the military strategist Basil Liddell-Hart.

Half-measures, he said, would not suffice against Nazi total war, and he insisted, rightly or wrongly, that bombing civilians is no worse than killing teenage soldiers.

Modern war is simply "frightful" in every way, and it is unhelpful, Orwell said, to draw fixed moral lines between different kinds of carnage.

But a total war of nuclear aggression in peacetime, to prevent future total wars? That, Orwell said, would be crackpot "realism" run amok.

More truly realistic is a possibility that Burnham dismisses out of hand—an attempt to "make democratic Socialism work...over a large area," which is most feasible, Orwell says, in "Western Europe plus Africa."

Of course, "the practical and psychological difficulties in the way are enormous...the apathy and conservatism of people everywhere, their unawareness of danger, their inability to imagine anything new...but it is a possible project if people really want it."

Twilight and Dawn

We owe the motto "*Pessimism of the intellect and optimism of the will*" to Antonio Gramsci. Few people have embodied that phrase more fully than George Orwell—and that, I believe, is the key to understanding him. He cherished few illusions about the hard world around him, but he also kept his fondest hopes alive. He was not only a utopian but a pragmatist. And it is precisely this duality that his critics find hardest to grasp. How could Orwell be both a socialist and a prophet of doom?

When Orwell embraced socialism, the very idea was under a cloud, thanks to Stalin's "Socialism in One Country" and Hitler's "National Socialism." Taking the stand he did required a stubborn refusal to disbelieve in democracy at a time when many people were sure it was doomed. Orwell knew the power of authoritarianism, but he refused to surrender to authoritarianism or appease authoritarians. What Malraux in 1946 called "tragic humanism" was Orwell's ethic as well. This was the ethic of those who knew human frailties too well to succumb to easy optimism, but who also refused to let terror triumph. Orwell's fidelity to this difficult ethic led him along a winding path. But his principles remained constant even as circumstances changed.

In Barcelona, he turned against Stalinism,

a stance he reaffirmed after the Stalin-Hitler pact. But when Hitler invaded Russia, Orwell supported the ensuing Soviet-British alliance, without softening his hostility to Stalinism. He and Koestler wanted to preserve this alliance, and peace, after the war.

When Zhdanov made that impossible, Orwell moved to the Hebrides and wrote a bleakly prophetic novel. He hoped that dystopia, viscerally imagined, could be averted.

Few of George Orwell's friends and admired fellow writers could sustain their hopefulness under the darkening skies of the early Cold War.

Nearly everyone in his milieu who could be called a tragic humanist, nearly everyone whom he had earlier praised as a utopian, now succumbed to pessimism. Optimism of the will was in short supply; lesser evils were gratefully accepted.

Koestler and Russell were just two of the many who gravitated to anti-Soviet liberalism. Koestler first moved in Cold War circles in 1948, during a visit to the United States. In 1950, he was the featured speaker at the inaugural conference of the Congress of Cultural Freedom—which was secretly funded by the CIA.

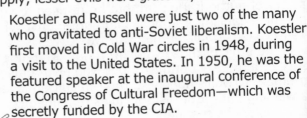

In 1955, Koestler retired into private life, much as Orwell had once predicted.

Russell, too, was active in the Congress of Cultural Freedom and other Cold War groups—and then, in the 1960s, he became an antiwar radical...

Where, if he had lived, would Orwell have wound up on this political map?

NICE   NAUGHTY

CLOCKWISE ● ORWELL, MARGARET STEWART, CHARLIE CHAPLIN, ISAAC DEUTSCHER, TOM DRIBERG, V. G. CHILDE, PETER SMOLLETT, E. H. CARR, KINGSLEY MARTIN, PAUL ROBESON, CELIA PAGET

Our best chance of answering this question comes from *Nineteen Eighty-Four* itself. We see here a concentrated critique of mendacity and authoritarianism—a critique which has now reverberated for generations. He denied early charges that he was attacking socialism, saying that, in fact, pseudo-socialist oligarchy—and modern oligarchies of all kinds—were his targets. He would have appreciated the irony in the fact that Russia's present rulers are universally called "oligarchs." And their Western equivalents, the aptly named 1%, would not have won his allegiance...

This is not to claim perfect consistency for Orwell. His attitude toward aerial bombing during the war bordered on cynical realism—and many people were surprised to learn, in the '90s, that in the final year of his life, Orwell named names. Asked by his friend Celia Paget to privately advise the Labour government about intellectuals who could be trusted to represent British interests, Orwell also furnished a list of nearly 40 figures he deemed unreliable—often accompanied by caustic judgments.

Many excuses have been offered by Orwell's admirers. He was seriously ill, Celia was a friend, he wished the Labour government well, British intelligence was just getting its feet wet in the Cold War. But it is hard not to see this as a moral lapse.

Just as *Nineteen Eighty-Four* was appearing in print, Orwell secretly accused fellow writers of "crypto-communism" and other political sins. He thus demonstrated by his own fallibility the difficulty of living up to the standards of his astringent ethic.

Past, Present, Future

Everyone whose sensibility has been touched by Orwell's serrated imagination, even if only by cultural osmosis, knows that despotism and double-speak have had few more effective adversaries.

Nearly eighty years after his death, Orwell's voice rings out across decades and generations against ruthless oligarchies and truthless propaganda.

And as much as we may feel that we continue to live in an Orwellian world, we should also recall that a great deal of what has happened since Orwell's death is, in a way, post-Orwellian.

Mass opposition to leader-worship, war-fever, and race-hatred was negligible in Orwell's lifetime. Only since the 1950s have truly mass movements tested their strength against war and prejudice. Only in the postwar period has leader-worship of the kind claimed by Stalin and Hitler fallen into disrepute. Pessimism of the intellect remains indispensable; but there are new grounds for optimism, as well.

KOESTLER AT
THE CONGRESS
FOR CULTURAL
FREEDOM
PODIUM
IN 1950

Orwell drifted apart from Koestler in his final years. He showed benign interest in Koestler's wanderings (to Palestine and France as well as to America) but he did not follow him into the Cold War barracks.

Just days after Orwell died, Koestler wrote a rueful testament to his friend's stubborn idealism, which was as accurate as it was defensive and condescending.

If George Orwell were to choose his own epitaph, Koestler guessed, he would probably quote Old Major's revolutionary anthem, from *Animal Farm*:

Rings shall vanish from our noses, and the harness from our back, ...
For that day we all must labour, though we die before it break;
Cows and horses, geese and turkeys,
all must toil for freedom's sake.

"Somehow," Koestler concluded, "Orwell really believed in this. It was this quaint belief which guided the rebel's progress, and made him so very lovable."